150 Waterfowling Tips,
Tactics & Tales

SPORTS AFIELD

150

Waterfowling
Tips, Tactics & Tales

by Chris Dorsey

Willow Creek ®
P R E S S

MINOCQUA, WISCONSIN

ALL CLIP ART/PHOTOS © 2002-2003 ARTTODAY.COM

Published by Willow Creek Press, P.O. Box 147, Minocqua, Wisconsin 54548

For information on other Willow Creek Press titles, call 1-800-850-9453 or visit www.willowcreekpress.com.

Library of Congress Cataloging-in-Publication Data
150 waterfowling tips, tactics & tales from Sports afield magazine.
  p. cm.
  ISBN 1-57223-594-2 (softcover : alk. paper)
1. Waterfowl shooting. 2. Hunting stories. I. Title: One hundred fifty waterfowling tips, tactics, and tales from Sports afield magazine. II. Sports afield.
  SK313 .A15 2002
  799.2'44--dc21

2002008233

Printed in the U.S.A.

Stories and Essays

The Legacy
of the Marsh Hunter

by Chris Dorsey

I N THE MARSH LIVES MANY TALES, AND FEW FORMS OF HUNTING ARE AS storied as waterfowling. For the generations of watermen who have plied their craft from coastal marshes to inland sloughs, there is a unique magnetism to the sport of duck and goose hunting. Waterfowling takes people to special places — settings made memorable by the painting of sun rays and the sound of whistling wings. The theater of a marsh is rife with wild characters and there is no better seat to witness such performances than that holiest of pulpits called the duck blind. That allure has drawn duck and goose hunters to

wetland cathedrals across America for generations.

There also is the compelling nature of the birds themselves, feathered gifts delivered by north winds. It takes but one awe-inspiring morning under a sky darkened by wildfowl to create a waterfowler. Part of the charm of waterfowling is that each bird carries with it a story. A hunter who holds a freshly taken duck in his hand possesses an artifact of the north. The duck might have come from some far away glacial pool, perhaps hatched in the shadow of migrating caribou or next to the paw print of a polar bear.

One can only imagine the perils of predators and weather that such a bird must have overcome before it visited one's blind.

The rich diversity of birds, too, provides the 'fowler with a close-up view of beautiful and varied creatures. Perhaps no duck rivals the majesty of the wood duck, a creature said to have been painted by the hand of God himself. Then there is the Harlequin duck, a bird whose stunning blue, white and russet plumage makes it appear overdressed for its murky surroundings. There are so many more — each bird being memorable for subtlety of its plumage or for its striking good looks.

Early Hunters

While hunting methods have evolved over the years, the spirit of the duck hunter remains a common thread in the fabric of wildfowling — past and present. The most notable — and inventive — of the early waterfowlers were the market gunners. While ruthless in their slaughter of ducks, geese, and swans, these profiteers continually developed more efficient ways of increasing their take. Many employed enormous punt guns, massive cannons mounted on skiffs. Such armament could raze whole flocks in a single shot. This ingenuity, coupled with better equipment, led to increased profits. As early as the 1870s, urbanites in New York and other tidewater communities could buy wildfowl from street vendors. A Forest & Stream article from the period listed prices paid for fowl: Swans, $2.75; canvasbacks, $1 a pair; and redheads, black ducks, and mallards, 75 cents a pair.

By the turn of the century, however, the toll exacted by market gunners was showing signs of lasting damage, for annual migrations began to dwindle. Experts from the period estimated that as many as 15,000 canvasbacks were being taken daily from the waters of Chesapeake Bay alone. It was a pace that cold not be sustained. Logbooks from waterfowling clubs across the country told the story as they recorded smaller and smaller harvests.

Sportsmen across America soon began calling for a moratorium on the use of punt guns and an end to market gunning altogether. In 1900, Congress responded by passing the Lacey Act, bringing the practice of market gunning to an end. Numerous other laws further protecting waterfowl were soon passed, and in 1913, the Weeks-Mclean bill became law, giving responsibility for managing migratory game birds to the U.S. Bureau of Biological Survey, the forerunner of the U.S. Fish and Wildlife Service. In 1935, the use of live decoys for waterfowl hunting was also banned.

The most important event of the period, however, was the great drought that spanned much of the nation's breadbasket. The decade of the 1930s was remembered for the "Dust Bowl" that turned once productive farmland and wildlife habitat into barren wastelands. The prolonged drought had a devastating effect on both people and wildlife. Duck and goose populations plummeted, and sportsmen and other conservationists desperately scrambled to resurrect waning bird numbers. In 1937, a group of concerned sportsmen incorporated a small but active organization called Ducks Unlimited. It was a move that would forever change the face of American waterfowl conservation. Funds raised by DU were sent to Ducks Unlimited Canada, the delivery arm of the organization, for work on the critical breeding grounds, primarily across the prairie provinces of Alberta, Saskatchewan, and Manitoba.

In the same year, the Pittman-Robertson Federal Aid in Wildlife Restoration Act was passed — thanks to the urging of concerned sportsmen — establishing an excise tax on sporting equipment sales. The "PR" Act, as it is known, has since generated billions of dollars for wildlife habitat restoration. The concept of the Federal Duck Stamp was also conceived in this decade, raising nearly $500 million to create waterfowl refuges across the country — to date, more than 4 million acres of waterfowl habitat have been purchased thanks to duck stamp funds.

The New Ethic: When President Franklin Roosevelt appointed a special presidential committee to develop recommendations to restore migratory waterfowl in 1934, he ushered-in the era of modern conservation. The commission included such notables as Aldo Leopold (widely regarded as the father of conservation) and Ding Darling, a Pulitzer Prize winning cartoonist who often lamented the destruction of waterfowl habitat in his syndicated illustrations. Darling, in fact, penned the first federal duck stamp in 1934. The notion that sportsmen must be stewards of the land and the wildlife that depends on it began to take widespread root.

Since that time, waterfowlers have been America's leading conservationists, instigating state stamps and taxes to help pay for sorely needed wildlife habitat. Since Ducks Unlimited's founding in 1937, for instance, the organization has raised more than $1 billion to conserve over 8 million acres of habitat. DU has also been instrumental in helping pass vital conservation provisions in such important legislation as the Conservation Reserve Program.

Such commitment to the resource is proof of the value waterfowlers place on their sport. With growing pressures to convert wetlands to crop fields and developments, every dawn punctuated by flocks of ducks and skeins of geese comes with a price. For those who live for sunrise over the cattails, however, securing the future for wildfowl is a way of paying homage to the past.

W hether you're hunting from a full pit blind, a half-pit, a boat, a shore blind, or if you're simply lying on the ground under a camo cover, there must be nothing "unnatural" about your appearance from the air. You can't have anything that shines or glares; this includes gunstocks and barrels, eyeglasses, spent shotshells, upward-turned faces, and ungloved hands. And your dog's lolling pink tongue is a dead giveaway too!

For waterfowl hunters, knowing when a bird is at 35 yards is vital. The most successful wingshooting is generally done at this distance, or closer, and shooting past 35 yards requires more forward allowance or lead. Estimating range in waterfowl hunting, however, is often tricky. Ducks and geese vary considerably in size, and when they are directly overhead, you do not have other references to help judge the distance. Try putting out a stick or other marker at 35 yards, and visualize an imaginary arc above you at that range. Similarly, place a decoy 35 yards away and vow not to shoot at any birds beyond it.

Biologists recognize 14 sub-species of Canada geese, ranging in size from the diminutive cackling goose, which averages 3.4 pounds, to the giant Canada, which can weigh 12 pounds or more.

"If I must chose among the sports that draw me into the open, it will be duck hunting. No other sport with rod or gun holds so much of mystery and drama.
The game comes out of the sky."
~Gordon MacQuarrie, "The Bluebills Died at Dawn."
(October '00, p.64)

Many species of puddle ducks migrate south when harsh weather moves in. Some species, both puddlers and diver, however, will hang around as long as open water and food are available.

Heavy waterfowling parkas and bulky gloves can make gunning difficult. Wear your foul-weather gear while practicing at the range before the season. It's also a good idea to get in some informal practice shooting from the kneeling and sitting positions you'll be in when the ducks are flying. For this, enlist a friend or two, find an area where you can safely shoot, and set up some duck-shooting situations using a hand trap or an inexpensive ground trap. And don't forget to toss some doubles, too.

"For the waterfowler who is brave enough to face the elements, there is no season like the late season."
~Winston March, circa 1910

Among the most celebrated of all waterfowling traditions, flooded timber duck hunting often requires aggressive calling, good camouflage, and effective concealment for success.

Bluebill populations have declined at a rate of 150,000 birds per year for the last 20 years.

Crows have the sharpest eyes in the avian world. They can glance down at you and tell you the name of your date for the senior prom. Observe the way crows react as they fly over your duck blind. If they swerve in their flight, it means you need to add camouflage. Fortunately, ducks are more trusting — but you still need to hide and hold still. And if you doubt that your shining face is a dead giveaway, try looking up at a crow that seconds before didn't know you were there. He'll tell you instantly by his actions that you've been made.

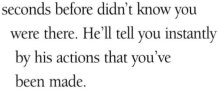

"They were swinging in now, a matter of seconds and they would be in range. Perennials, storm windows, fertilizers and shrubbery, what piddling mediocre stuff.
This was worth dying for."
~Sigurd Olsen, "A Shift in the Wind," (August '01, p.67)

A common cause of vertical wingshooting misses is failure to keep the cheek against the stock. But the real culprit may be your hat interfering with the sighting plane, making you lift your head. A brim too long or pulled down too low across the eyes makes you unconsciously pick your head up to see down the barrel. When your head comes up, your cheek comes off the stock, and you miss high.

When you first see ducks far off, use the highball or hail call. After they've started toward the decoy spread, switch to contented hen sounds such as the three-note greeting call, the single-note quack, and the feeding chuckle. One school of calling says to keep at it until the birds have their wings locked. Another school says as long as they are getting closer, stay quiet. The good callers prefer the former, the rest of us the latter. But there are other considerations. If it's a windy, blustery day and ducks are responding well, call heavy right down to the water. When it's calm and warm, the birds can get skittish and flare off from the call. Adjust your calling accordingly.

When marshes freeze, look for birds feeding in grainfields and loafing in creeks and rivers. Large reservoirs also hold ducks, since holes stay open in the ice. At this time, a float trip down an open river can put you into the birds.

When hunting waterfowl on public lands near the start of the season, call more aggressively than you would on private lands. The most skilled caller is usually the one who lures in the most game, and two callers are better than one. And don't be skimpy with the decoys, either. Big rigs will outdraw small rigs in areas where ducks are normally concentrated, such as around refuges. The opposite of this is true later in the season when the ducks have been hunted and are decoy- and call-shy. Now, cut back on your calling and the number of decoys in your spread.

After you've shot at a flock of ducks and, more likely, geese, remain hidden and give a series of fast, loud comeback calls. As unlikely as it seems, occasionally the birds will swing back and give you another try. This will more often work early in the season before the ducks have wised up and also on unsophisticated birds recently down from the northern Canadian provinces.

A Brief History of the Gear

by Chris Dorsey

THE FORERUNNERS OF MODERN SYNTHETIC DECOYS RANGED from stacks of seaweed to piles of rocks. An early decoy made of a combination of rushes and feathers was discovered in a Nevada cave in 1924. The creation clearly resembled a canvasback and was estimated to date from A.D. 800.

By the mid-19th century, however, live decoys were in widespread use — especially along Atlantic tidewaters. These "trained" birds not only provided lifelike movement but called other unsuspecting fowl as well. As one might surmise, the live birds were highly effective in duping passing ducks and geese. For market gunners, however, live decoys weren't practical, for they were too difficult to manage in large numbers. That ushered in the era of the wooden decoy.

The carved decoys of yesteryear so often sought after by modern collectors are the creations of market gunners. Compare a list of famous decoy carvers with a roster of market gunners and you will find numerous redundancies, for the two are nearly identical. In order to concentrate large flocks of ducks, market gunners needed huge decoy spreads. The early decoys — called

"Blocks" because of their rough forms — were mostly carved of white cedar, a wood common to the Northeast.

In 1935, the use of live decoys was banned altogether, creating an instant demand for artificial decoys and calls. Many of the early duck calls were difficult to blow and were often referred to as "tongue-pinchers." Philip Olt, however, the founder of the venerable P.S. Olt Call Company, was a duck call pioneer and made scores of improvements on the early metal reed calls. What is surprising is that the origins of the American duck call are found in the Mississippi Flyway, not the Atlantic Flyway so celebrated as the cradle of our nation's fowling legacy. One expla-nation for this is the fact that many of the ducks hunted on the east coast were sea ducks and, thus, didn't readily react to the sound of calls anyway. Conversely, the Mississippi Flyway is the home of the mallard, and this vocal species readily responds to calling.

While advancements were being made in decoys and calls, gun designers such as John Browning were also busy innovating new shotguns for waterfowlers. Browning's Auto 5 — created in 1899 — became the standard issue for turn-of-the-century waterfowlers who raved over the gun's reliability and effectiveness. Prior to that, Browning developed the Model 1897 pump shotgun for Winchester, another popular model among waterfowlers.

Perhaps no other pump gun ever achieve the widespread acceptance of the Winchester Model 12. It became the standard by which all other pumps were judged, and was used for a variety of feathered and furred game.

Along with improvements in gun design came better cartridges. In 1924, Remington's James Burns invented the first ever noncorrosive primer. Within two years, shells with noncorrosive primers were on the market. This development meant that hunters no longer had to clean their gun barrels after only a few firings. In 1960, plastic shotshell hulls were introduced. This made it possible for hunters to reload their own shells using components.

Of the scores of inventive craft used to reach favorite fowling waters, none is as revered in history as the Barnegat Bay Sneak Box. This low-drafting boat allowed hunters to reach shallow inlets throughout tidal sloughs. The craft was so popular that it remains in use even today as a handful of the boat's devotees still build them.

There is seemingly no limit to the kinds of rigs employed by waterfowlers. From dories to sloops and from skiffs to pirogues, watermen have used a wide variety of specialized craft for generations. Modern synthetic fibers and special construction make waterfowling infinitely safer today than it was 60 or 70 years ago, but technological advances are no substitute for discretion when it comes to facing rough waters in a small craft.

"Waterfowling holds some special magic, something available only from the world of water and wind, of mud stiff with cold, of black dogs and long guns."
~Michael McIntosh, "Gunning the Grand Passage" (September '01, p.73)

To attract the most geese to your spread, put out a majority of decoys in resting or lie-down positions. This attracts waterfowl more readily than decoys in alert or feeding positions. The relaxed demeanor of your spread tells the approaching birds that everything is peaceful and safe down below.

The Canada goose is indeed a dedicated parent.
During the 28-day incubation period,
an adult goose may leave its nest for as few as
10 hours out of 672. Some geese have even
been known to starve on the nest.

M allards, the country's best-known ducks, are also the most widely distributed ducks in the world. Except for the muscovy, the mallard is the ancestor of all our domestic ducks.

It takes six live geese to produce one pound
of the best pillow feathers.

anada geese mate for life (up to 20 years), and the same pair may nest in almost the same spot each year. They have such great concern for each other that if one bird dies, the other is frequently reluctant to leave the area. During the next season, the survivor will usually find another mate. Before we get too anthropomorphic, however, there is a biological reason for this. Geese nest in the north and the birds must mate, nest, and brood eggs; the chicks must then hatch and grow to near-adult size in time for the autumn migration, or die. If courtship were added to this regimen, and given the size a goose must grow to before it can make long flights, there would not be enough time for all of it to take place, and the last stage wouldn't be completed — the chicks growing to migration size. It's simply more efficient to take one mate for life and eliminate annual courtship. In addition, both parents rear the brood, something the polygamous species do not do.

There is speculation about the "V" formation used in flight. Some studies suggest turbulence created by the leader makes flying behind easier. As such, there are continuous changes of "leaders" to spell the one first cutting the air. For a little fun, the next time you see a V of geese go over, ask your companion why one side of the V is almost always longer. When he pleads ignorance, tell him it's because one side of the V has more geese in it.

Male geese will stage royal battles for a female, approaching with necks outstretched, hissing loudly, and pecking and jabbing with their long necks like swordsmen, while they flail with powerful wings. When the loser beats a hasty retreat, the winner loudly proclaims his victory, dipping his head underwater to preen as he returns to the female.

If you're floating a river and spot ducks far downstream, pull to shore and send one hunter looping down to stalk them from below. He'll likely get a shot as they flush and so will the person hunkering down hidden next to the boat upstream as the birds fly past.

When jumpshooting ducks along rivers and streams, stay back 15 to 30 yards from the bank if the cover is sparse, looping up close every 40 to 60 yards to check for ducks. If vegetation is thick, work closer to the bank using cover such as brush, logs, and trees as you sneak along. If you have a choice, pick water with lots of brush or trees on the shore, plus bends and elevated banks. All of these qualities help you sneak up on the birds for close 20-35-yard shots. Use an improved-cylinder

choke and No. 2-4 steel shot. Hold above the ducks when they jump; most jump-shots are missed under.

Teal hunting depends on many factors, weather and water being the most important. Teal prefer extremely shallow water, mud-flat sloughs, marshes, reservoirs, ponds, and lakes. Changing water levels from autumn rains will affect the preferred areas of the little birds.

"With 7X eyesight . . . and wisdom born of a long lifespan, an old Canada gander is the waterfowl equivalent of a 12-point buck; he didn't get that way being stupid."
~Steve Smith, Hunting Ducks and Geese, (September '01, p.97)

Teal typically tend to bunch up more than other ducks on the water, so decoys can be placed close to one another. A more open spread, however, creates a bigger visual impact from a distance. Teal, like all waterfowl, land into the wind and the decoy set should take advantage of this, describing a "J" or "C" shape with a landing pocket in front of the gunners.

W hen calling teal, mallard calls can be used to capture the attention of teal, but calls should be fairly sparse and soft. Try soft quacks, feeding chuckles, sit-down calls, and muffled, high-pitched hail calls with a mallard call. Teal make squeaky, high-pitched peeps, so a pintail call or a dog whistle are effective tools to draw their attention. After calling them in, don't count on an easy shoot. Their habit of twisting, darting, turning, and flying at speeds

of 50 miles per hour or more through brush and trees makes them extremely challenging. Select one bird in the flock, and follow through. Once hit, a teal is not a hard bird to bring down.

Canada geese are creatures of habit. When they find a field of grain to feast on, they'll return as long as grain remains and they aren't molested, or until harsh weather drives them farther south. Watch for concentrations to build in the fields during afternoon hours, and stay until hunting hours are over to make sure they are not disturbed; if they are not, chances are good they will return the next morning to feed. Pattern more than one field as a backup and before sunup the next morning, get on the field and search out the exact area the geese were grazing the previous afternoon. Fresh droppings will mark the spot. Set the bulk of your decoys in this spot (downwind of your shooting position), and be sure to leave an opening for a landing zone in the portion of the decoy layout farthest downwind. Early in the season, you can get away with one or two dozen decoys, but later, during migration, six to 10 dozen may be required.

When jump-shooting ducks along rivers and streams, try using a call every now and then. You might get birds that you hadn't seen to respond and reveal their location. At times, they might even fly or swim down toward you into shooting range, where you can flush them.

Hunting from a conventional blind during the late season may no longer be the ticket. You might have to get more mobile, go to areas ducks are using, set up a temporary blind, boat blind, or portable blind, and throw out a smaller decoy spread. Location of the blind would be best on, say, island points or points of a river or lake. Wind has a lot to do with location.

Going Mobile
by Chris Dorsey

TRAVEL THE COUNTRY IN SEARCH OF THE PERFECT DUCK
blind and you will come to the conclusion — as I have — that duck
hunters in America build more structures than Habitat for Humanity.
Some of these creations are concrete and steel bunkers complete with
electric grills and gas heat. What they provide in comfort, however,
they often lack in gunning opportunities. In my experience, there is a correlation
between the size and permanence of a blind and the number of birds that will visit the
adjacent spread. By contrast, many of my most memorable waterfowling days were
spent simply lying among the decoys or behind the flimsiest of temporary hides.

There is a simple explanation for this: If you want to enjoy consistent gunning, go
to where the birds want to land. This approach is far easier than trying to continually coax birds to your permanent blind from which passing birds have been shot at
since opening day. I've spent too many days in luxurious blinds watching ducks and
geese sail past without even taking a glance at our decoy spreads. Hunters who
invest in such structures are relying on a steady influx of new birds to provide
consistent shooting, for birds quickly learn to associate trouble with static decoy
spreads. The problem is that it often takes major weather systems to move birds, so
if you don't have a change in weather, you're not apt to have many new, gullible
birds to fool.

For hunters who are willing to sacrifice comfort for more consistent gunning,
mobility is the solution. A growing number of waterfowlers are discovering the virtues
of small decoy spreads and ever-changing scenery. Scouting bird movements become
critical to success, for if you can find the fields or marshes in which ducks or geese

want to feed or loaf, you will be on your way to a memorable outing. Waterfowl movements will change throughout the season, often reflecting the progression of grain harvests and water conditions. Around refuge areas, for instance, Canada and snow geese are never far behind combines harvesting corn, wheat, soybeans, or rice. Find a field occupied by feeding birds at dusk and you'll likely find them in the same spot the following morning — you have only to arrive ahead of the visiting flights with your decoy invitations in place before dawn to lure them within shotgun range.

There are a variety of small, portable, coffin-style blinds that work well to conceal you among the decoy spread. With the creation of new and better camouflage patterns for field and marsh gunning — Advantage Wetlands, Mossy Oak Shadow

Grass, Backland, and Cornstalk to name a few — there is less need for blinds than ever before. In dry conditions, simply bring a shovel along to scrape out a depression in the earth to fit the contour of your body. This is not only a comfortable way to rest in the field, but will keep your profile below the grain stubble — key to not being spotted by approaching ducks or geese.

When going mobile for waterfowl, I prefer to use silhouette decoys because they are lighter and easier to transport than their full-body or shell counterparts. As few as two dozen blocks will usually suffice if you've found a location in which the birds have been consistently feeding. If you're lying among the decoys, position a few of the silhouettes around you to help mask your movements and break up your form. In shallow flooded fields, coffin blinds are extremely effective, keeping you both hidden and dry.

The mobile waterfowler can also take advantage of jumpshooting opportunities found on hidden potholes, marshes, or streams. During the early season when hunting pressure is most intense, ducks and geese will often find secluded hideouts in which to escape the barrage of guns. I have a couple of favorite ponds — one is located in the midst of a 2,000 acre corn field, the other is in a stand of timber about one mile off the nearest road. These are just the kinds of places that few people discover, and that ducks love to frequent when they're forced off much larger marshes located nearby. If I haven't collected enough birds for the pot after a morning in my marsh blind, I stop by these hidden haunts and invariably surprise loafing ducks.

If access is a problem and you're confined to a given area throughout the season, fear not, for there are several simple steps that will improve your success. The first is to construct multiple blinds so that birds aren't continually encountering hunters in familiar locations — for instance, you might locate blinds at opposite ends of a field. Repositioning your decoys is another approach that makes your spread more realistic. Too many hunters decide to leave their frost covered blocks in the field in the same position throughout the season. If you don't want to go to the trouble of moving your blocks, at least keep a broom in the blind to sweep off the frost or snow that accumulates on your decoys. Shiny decoys will spook most birds.

For the wildfowler who tastes the virtues of mobility, however, there's no returning to blind luck

Remember that all waterfowl prefer to land into the wind. If you have some flooded timber around you or a bunch of trees around a pothole or the point of an island, the ducks are going to swing around downwind to come into your decoys. This needs to be taken into consideration because you do not want to set up so that they have a hurdle to overcome before they can land in your set. Make it easy for the birds on their approach. There should be nothing between you and them that might make them uncomfortable or hesitant. Wind change may mean you have to move to the opposite side of the island or point to give the birds an unobstructed path to your spread.

In cold waterfowling weather, it is important to be comfortable. Dress in layers to keep from overheating when putting out decoys, rowing, hiking to a blind, or doing other chores. Then add layers as you begin to cool. If you are boating on big water, wear a floatation suit, which provides extra insulation along with the safety protection of a life jacket. Carry a full set of clothing in a waterproof bag if you're in a boat, or in your blind or car if it is close enough.

Late-season waterfowl hunting means rougher water, colder wind, and longer shots. Break an oar in an offshore wind, and you've got big troubles. Bring a good anchor; retie lines; carry spare gloves; and shoot heavier loads. Be aware of the bulk you're hauling; four dozen decoys weigh more than you think, particularly when you add a blind, retriever, hunting buddy, gun, binoculars, lunch, thermos, and other gear.

Wide-open spaces should not intimidate waterfowl hunters, though with so much water staring back at you, just finding ducks can at first be mind-boggling. The same depth charts you use for fishing may serve as a helpful starting point. Ducks frequent the shallow, shoal areas where they can feed on aquatic vegetation. One to five feet of water is about right for puddle ducks, four to 15 feet or more for divers.

Explore hidden spots from view, like setbacks and the back sides of islands, as well as areas distant from boat ramps and access points.

Use decoys and calls that match the species you find while scouting. Remember that mallard decoys will draw other puddlers, such as blacks and pintails, and bluebill decoys will do the same for shoreline divers such as buffle-heads and goldeneyes. If you're hunting bay divers such as scaup, canvasbacks, or redheads, any of the three will do.

The bigger the water, the more decoys you'll need. Drawing in ducks from any distance takes many decoys, but you can cut back by setting up in an area ducks have been using. The same applies to your duck call — when they're high and far, you want to get on the horn in a hurry.

There are some weather conditions that can help a duck hunt immensely. Fog, low cloud cover, and sleet or drizzle seem to soften horizons and images. A breeze imparts movement to the blocks and sometimes keeps the birds moving as well. Some strategies call for wind to blow at your back, but a left-to-right or right-to-left breeze is all the better. This way, approaching ducks see nothing but water and decoys, because the birds always land into the wind. With the wind at your back, the ducks are approaching straight at you, and you're more likely to be visible.

Etiquette of the Blind

by George Bird Grinnell

S INCE IT OFTEN HAPPENS THAT TWO GUNNERS MAY SHOOT OUT of the same box or the same blind, it is evident that to avoid wasting shots, and to get the most satisfaction out of the shooting, certain rules governing the conduct of each man must be observed. These unwritten laws will be taught most men by their own good feeling and proper instincts; but, on the other hand, it often happens that a very young man in the blind, carried away by excitement and enthusiasm, may do things which in cooler blood he would not think of doing, and which may prove very annoying to his companion.

The laws governing such shooting are well understood by all men of experience, but since each one of us must have made a beginning in shooting, it will perhaps be easier for the inexperienced if some of these laws are here noted.

These unwritten rules are based on the principle that where two men shoot together they are not rivals, each striving to outdo the other, but are partners, working for the common good, which in this case means the success of the day. It is therefore important that no shots should be wasted and that each one should do all in his power to bring to bag the birds which come within shot. Besides this, of course, there are the general laws of good manners, which govern in such a case just as they should in other relations in life.

It is therefore to be understood that the two men should never interfere with each other; they should never fire at the same bird at the same time, and if several come together, the gunners should understand without words which bird belongs to each.

If a single duck comes up that man should shoot at it from whose side it comes, and he should have the opportunity to use both barrels before his companion shoots. If the ducks come constantly from one side, as often they will come from the leeward, turns should be taken on the single birds. If they come from the leeward, the man to leeward should kill first, but if this is followed by another single, he should sit back in the blind and let the windward man kill the duck. Of course, in case of a miss with both barrels, the man who has not shot is at liberty to do what he can toward killing the bird. If two or three, or more, birds come up to the decoys, from any quarter, the man who is to leeward should shoot the bird or birds on his side, and the man to windward those on his.

Sometimes three birds will come up, let us say, from the leeward; the leading bird would naturally be taken by the windward man, while the man to leeward would take the second one, and the third would be anybody's bird. A natural exclamation from the leeward man would be, under such circumstances, "You take the one in the lead!" but before the birds get up to the point where they would be shot at, the bird which was leading may have dropped back to second place. In such a case there is a possibility of a misunderstanding, for, if the windward man imagined that his companion referred to the individual duck that was in the lead, and which is now in second place, both men may shoot at this duck. Of course, no such blunder should ever occur. When one speaks of the leading duck he does not mean the particular duck that is leading at that moment, but the duck which is ahead when the shots are fired We have more than once seen a blunder of this kind take place, by which one or more shots were lost.

Under no circumstances will a thoughtful man, with proper instincts, shoot at a bird that properly belongs to his companion. Under no circumstances whatever will he shoot across his companion's face; and if your gunning companion be guilty of such a breach as this, he should never again have an opportunity to shoot in the blind with you.

It is not customary for men who are not well acquainted with each other to shot in the same blind, but if, by any misfortune, a gunner should find himself in a blind with a man who evidently is so selfish that he wants to kill all the birds, no matter from which direction they may come, he should leave the blind on the very first opportunity, and decline to return to it, or ever again to shoot with this person. Characteristics such as this, which would never be seen under the ordinary conditions of life, sometimes manifest themselves in the blind, and I know of one or two men, who have high reputations as sportsmen and high standing in the community, with whom, under no circumstances, would I share a blind or a box.

Most men, however, do not intentionally impose on their companions, and many, who under stress of excitement will do things which are not fair, and which they should not do, may be checked by a quiet word, and taught by a little precept and a good deal of example to act in the blind as men of good breeding should act everywhere.

There are few things which contribute more to a man's contentment than to have with him in the blind a cheerful, good-natured, generous companion. There is nothing which so greatly detracts from the pleasure of shooting as to shoot with one who does not show a reasonable amount of self-control, and who wants all the shots, or claims all the birds. And so, unless you have as a sharer of your blind some one whom you thoroughly know, and have confidence in, it is far better for you to shoot alone.

⤙—⟡—◯—⟡—⤚

"They were swinging in now, a matter of seconds and they would be in range. Perennials, storm windows, fertilizers and shrubbery, what piddling mediocre stuff. This was worth dying for." ~Sigurd Olsen, "A Shift in the Wind," (August '01, p.67)

⤙—⟡—◯—⟡—⤚

For late season puddle ducks, keep blinds to a minimum size. Ducks will remember what their late-autumn surroundings looked like, and they are not big on changes. Divers and puddlers also avoid objects rising above horizons, thus the popularity of layout boats and other low-profile blinds.

❦

How can you avoid shooting hens when waterfowling in poor light conditions, where it's difficult to differentiate between the sexes? It's possible to be fooled by the dark breast of a mature hen. Look for the drake's white ring and tail feathers as well as the yellow bill, all of which stand out in low light. Sound is also a giveaway; hens quack and call, while drakes emit low, guttural *wwhankss*. Drakes neither quack nor call.

For a great combination float in the fall, consider going after squirrels and ducks. If one quarry is in short supply, there's usually enough of the other to make up for it. Use a drab-painted canoe, johnboat, or rubber raft, and drape some brush over the bow with a rope. The person in the stern should steer while the one in the bow shoots. Switch after a predetermined number of shots, hits, or length of time. Never should both parties attempt to shoot at the same time. And be watchful of any houses or dwellings nearby, observing your state's safety zone if there is one.

The next time you buy bread stuffing or shaped potato chips in one of those red canisters, save it. Wiped and aired out, it makes a convenient waterproof container. Charts, licenses, registration cards, instructions, user's manuals — all slide neatly into the container. Just keep it capped; should it fall overboard on the way to your duck blind, you can easily spot the bright red canister floating.

A slow moving, narrow creek with plenty of bends is ideal for float hunting. If it flows through farm fields or an oak grove, so much the better; acorns in the water draw wood ducks. Choose a section of stream away from a highway: It's safer, and ducks prefer such secluded places. The key is to hug the shore, using bends to hide your downstream approach.

Late-season ducks seldom stray from their migration path, so proximity to a flyway or major food source (such as a flooded grainfield) becomes increasingly important as fall rolls on. Early or late, expect mostly puddle ducks — teal, woodies, shovelers, mallards, and blacks if you live in the Northeast. Puddle ducks tip-up for their food and tend to sit on the inside of a bend — the slipslope — where the water is shallow, the current minimal, and the weeds (food) substantial. Jumping ducks is like hunting grouse: you can flush one anywhere, but some spots seem to hold more than their share of them.

When shooting from the bow of a canoe, you're limited to a swinging radius of not much more than 90 degrees. If you're a right-handed shooter, the radius centers on your left shoulder; if you're a lefty, the right shoulder. Trouble occurs when the creek bends away from the hunter's shooting radius — for instance, to the right for a right-handed shooter. A duck flushes to the right, and the shot patters harmlessly to water well behind the bird. Enter the stern paddler; it's up him to "present" the creek to the gunner and push the bow to the right so the gunner can swing on the duck.

Forget the early morning hours. Jump-shoot small streams, backwater swamps, and flooded timber during the late morning and early afternoon. Ducks can often be found loafing at these times between the morning and evening feedings.

N ever approach a location directly if you're stalking a
stream or river on foot. Pause, crouching on your
hands and knees if necessary, to listen for nearby
ducks. Look ahead and take note of ripples on the water, which
might be made by feeding waterfowl.

J ump-shoot with
"one duck, one
shot" in mind.
Pick out a single
among the flushing
numbers and make
a clean kill.

There are a number of ways to retrieve downed ducks. You can use a landing net to dip them from the water and into the boat. You can cast a bass plug with treble hooks and reel the bird in. Or you can use the tried-and-true method preferred by thousands: Get a good retriever and train him.

The Nova Scotia Duck Tolling Retriever

by Chris Dorsey

OCCASIONALLY IN NATURE THERE EXIST ANIMALS SO unique that scientists have difficulty classifying them — the duck-billed platypus comes to mind, part mammal, part amphibian. In the canine world, perhaps no breed is as unique as the Nova Scotia Duck Tolling Retriever, a name that reads like the title of a scholarly paper. This breed has gained notoriety because it acts as both a decoy and a retriever. "Toll" comes from the Middle English word tollen, which means to lure or entice.

How, you might ask, does the dog do this? The foxlike dog runs up and down the bank of a lake, river, or marsh. Rafts of swimming ducks or geese, often inquisitive of such movement on shore, swim closer to investigate. I've seen this phenomenon with a wide variety of breeds along the shoreline of park lakes.

Upon spotting the dog, ducks and geese often swim 30 or 40 yards from the dog, sensing they are still a safe distance from the dog. Fact is, they are safe from the dog, but not from a gun. In a waterfowling situation, a hunter might be hidden in a blind just behind the dog as it runs up and down the bank. As the birds swim within shotgun range, the hunter surprises them and enjoys a jump shoot of sorts. Historically, such a tactic was practiced in England and other parts of Europe, where foxlike dogs were used to toll fowl into nets. The history of this breed is largely a mystery, though some experts believe the dog probably originated in Holland or England. Early Scottish settlers probably brought descendants of the breed to Nova Scotia, and many theories abound about what other breeds might have contributed to the Nova Scotia Duck Tolling Retriever.

The breed enjoys a small but loyal following and its tenacious but loveable nature make it well suited for a variety of work — not simply retrieving. Because of its compact dimensions, the breed moves easily in the uplands and is said to quarter much like a spaniel. Though it lacks the size (averaging 40 to 50 pounds) to easily tackle large geese and brant, it is nevertheless a reliable retriever. Though long distance retrieves are a challenge for the tolling dog, they efficiently handle short to mid-range retrieves, and they fit comfortably into boats, blinds, and canoes.

Because of their heavy coats, these dogs have won favor among many waterfowlers residing in cold climates. Seemingly unfazed by freezing temperatures and icy waters, the tolling dog eagerly undertakes virtually any cold water retrieve. While more independent than Labs, the tolling dog is purported to be a loyalist to its master.

While the AKC has yet to recognize the Nova Scotia Duck Tolling Retriever as an official breed, the Canadian Kennel Club, the United Kennel Club, and the International Kennel Club will all register the breed. In the U.S., the breed is sponsored by its own association (not surprisingly, the Nova Scotia Duck Tolling Retriever Club) that conducts a series of field trials (which include tolling) and keeps its own registry.

While the AKC has yet to recognize the Nova Scotia Duck Tolling Retriever as an official breed, the Canadian Kennel Club, the United Kennel Club, and the International Kennel Club will all register the breed. In the U.S., the breed is sponsored by its own association (not surprisingly, the Nova Scotia Duck Tolling Retriever Club) that conducts a series of field trials (which include tolling) and keeps its own registry.

Sit tight after flushing ducks and taking a shot. Sometimes flushed waterfowl will regroup in the same location.

To make plucking easier, use dishwashing detergent mixed with boiling water in a large picnic cooler. It might not sound like an ordinary duck-plucking technique, but it works. First, cut off the wings and submerge the duck with a stick to wet all of the feathers. Put the lid on the cooler, seal tightly, and let the duck steam for about 15 minutes. Remove the duck and let

it cool so you don't burn your fingers; the feathers should come off easily. Be sure to rinse the plucked duck thoroughly. There will be no detergent taste after you cook it.

When hunting teal, look for shallow, still water. Teal prefer to feed in water less than a foot deep. Newly-flooded wetland vegetation is attractive to them. They also fly rivers looking for calm, shallow areas.

Winter's opportunities are found where waterfowl concentrate around the remaining areas of food and water. The colder the weather, the more food waterfowl need to maintain body temperature, and so the more actively they will feed when they can find a source of food. Locate such a spot — corn that's been left standing or winter wheat that's coming up are prime areas.

Winds, floods, and tides bring hazards to marine wingshooting that many hunters might not realize. If you're hunting ducks or geese in tidal basins along bays or at the mouths of rivers, be sure you have a tide table handy, and note landmarks so you can beat a quick retreat from rising waters. Soft mud in these areas can also be dangerous; if you get stuck and find yourself sinking, most experts recommend that you fall on you back and try to squirm your way to firmer ground. Along creeks and rivers, many hunters wear the instantly inflatable vests made popular by fishermen. In all cases, it's wise to wear wool or other fabrics that conserve body heat even when thoroughly wet. Hypothermia is probably the most common threat wildfowlers face.

"Waterfowling holds some special magic, something available only from the world of water and wind, of mud stiff with cold, of black dogs and long guns."
~Michael McIntosh, "Gunning the Grand Passage"
(September '01, p.73)

If geese are not coming in to your calls and decoys, try waving a small black flag. This may or may not look to other geese like a goose flapping its wings before settling down; in any event, it adds life to the spread, often attracting birds that would otherwise fly on past. Once they start coming toward the spread, put the flag down and remain motionless, unless the birds are educated, in which case they may need to be flagged in all the way.

When it comes to placing decoys, there are few things to consider. First, a duck's predators generally come from shore, so he wants a buffer between the land and himself. The first decoys should be placed five to 10 yards from the blind so the rest of the spread remains within range. Ducks often like to set down just outside the decoys, so the far edge of your spread should be within effective killing range. Second, divide the decoys into two bunches, leaving a landing site between them for ducks to fall into. Finally, since ducks like to land into the wind, set up with the wind blowing across or at your back, not into your face. After that, good calling may get them to notice your spread; then it's all up to the ducks!

A duck blind can offer the comforts of home, but many hunting areas do not allow permanent blinds. Under such conditions, most waterfowl hunters hunker down under a tree or in other vegetation, and it's usually in the water or mud. This is fine for a little while, but the shifting, muddy bottom can lead to fatigue. To avoid this discomfort, bring a plank or small sheet of wood to lay down as a platform. Or, for additional comfort, construct a short bench with two or three braced 2x4s for legs, three feet in length, to be sunk into the mud. You can sit on

this as on a piano bench or straddle it if it's narrow enough. The plank and the bench will make the marsh a more comfortable place to spend a morning.

Are the ducks flaring? Try moving your dekes in, not out. If it's the decoys they don't like, you may gain an extra 20 or 30 feet before they shy away. Strange as it may seem, another solution is to wade into your spread. There's no doubt incoming flocks will see you, but if you're still, you may be ignored. If, on the other hand, you've determined there's something about your blind they don't like, try wading to the opposite bank (if it's close enough), hunkering down in the brush, and hunting from there. The next flock that comes by may flare right into your lap.

Tie a cord to a "feeder" or "tip-up" decoy, run it through an anchor below (half a plastic soda bottle filled with concrete works well), and then back to the blind. Yank on the cord when birds are working the decoys. Great on quiet water, ponds, and sloughs. When hunting on creeks or small streams, make your own "swimming" decoy by drilling a hole an inch or two behind the front of the keel and attaching the anchor line there. In any kind of current, the front of the keel will act like the lip on a bass plug, making the decoy "swim" from side to side. Likewise, tossing something for your retriever to fetch can draw attention to your spread. The dog's head moving through the decoys looks like a swimming duck. (Sort of.)

Reservoirs, big lakes, bays, and sounds are great spots for duck hunting, especially at the beginning of the season when birds are unwary. But puddle ducks wise up after a few days of gunning pressure, and either gather into huge, unapproachable rafts out in the middle of the water or leave altogether to search out smaller, more secluded waters. If you want good hunting, do the same.

Crying Fowl
by Chris Dorsey

T O PARAPHRASE MARK TWAIN, THE DIFFERENCE BETWEEN THE right call and nearly the right call is the same as that between lightning and the lightning bug. Indeed, there are many subtleties to calling wildfowl, variances that would take years for a hunter to learn on his own. Fortunately, by following the advice of these seasoned waterfowlers, you can dramatically shorten the learning curve and find yourself face to face with flocks of approaching birds.

For World Champion duck caller and guide Buck Gardner, successfully calling ducks is about more than just sounding like the birds. "You have to choose the right location and be where the ducks want to go," he says. "You also need to match your calling with an alluring decoy spread if you want to draw the birds close to the gun."

Finding a location where the ducks want to be is simply a matter of scouting the birds' daily movements between feeding and roosting areas. Even the most convincing call recital will have little effect if a caller is not located where ducks want to light. Much of the intrigue of waterfowling is trying to decipher what a duck or a goose is thinking, how it perceives its environment, and what makes one bird plunge headlong toward your decoys while another doesn't even hasten a second glance. There are, to be sure, many mysteries inside the acorn-sized brain of a duck — many that are destined to remain unsolved. No matter how confident you might be that you know what a duck is going to do, there will always be birds that defy prediction. The more you hunt ducks, to be certain, the more you come to appreciate the many mysteries of wildfowling.

Despite their idiosyncrasies, ducks routinely communicate through a series of vocalizations ranging from quacks to whistles. Even ducks that do not quack — such as wood ducks, teal, and pintail — often respond to mallard quacks, so the mallard call is far and away the most popular duck call available. "There are four basic calls hunters should use to call ducks," says Gardner, "the feed chuckle, comeback, high-ball, and lonesome hen."

To understand when you should use each of these calls, picture yourself seated in your favorite blind. Now, imagine a high flock of mallards coursing overhead, silhouetted against an amber morning sky. This is the ideal moment to greet them with the highball or hail call. This call consists of a long series of quacks that, when blown properly, develop almost a ringing sound. After several loud quacks, the call should taper off. Though you'll never hear a hen mallard make such a sound, the call does serve as an attention-grabber. Gardner likens such a call to the use of flags when trying to decoy geese. "A flag doesn't look like a goose," he acknowledges, "but it does get geese to notice decoys from a long distance and the same is true of the highball."

Despite the fact that the highball, at close range, can be especially overbearing, it's a great call to employ when trying to get distant birds to examine your decoy spread. As a rule, the higher the ducks, the louder you'll need to blow your highball. Though ducks might not respond to your 10- 15-
note highball immediately, watch for any deviation in their flight — your first clue that the birds might be inspecting your decoys. If the ducks show no variance in their flight, concentrate on locating and calling other birds, for those ducks already have a different destination in mind.

If, however, the high-flyers separate from the flock to take a closer look at your stool, you'll want to begin a series of six to eight hen quacks in varying pitches to present the illusion that several ducks are calling. "Reading" a duck's in-flight behavior takes considerable experience, and only time in a blind observing how ducks respond to other ducks and to calling will give you an appreciation for duck habits. Studying duck behavior is something that can be practiced year-round in many areas, for local parks often host resident mallard flocks that provide an up-close look at how ducks behave and communicate. As ducks pass through your area during the spring migration, also consider returning to your favorite blind to practice your calling techniques.

Once a flock of ducks decides to approach your blocks, you'll want to employ the lonesome hen call, a protracted series of quacks that have a similar tone and volume. By rapidly blowing the call, you can add a sense of pleasing or urgency to your message. This is a call commonly made by hen mallards to entice other ducks to land near them. Though ducks often look for a place to feed, drakes continually seek the company of hens; thus, they can be especially receptive to a seductive lonesome hen call.

As ducks cup their wings to set over your decoys, you'll want to blow an assurance call to coax them even closer to your blocks. For most waterfowlers, this means blowing the feed chuckle, a rapid series of clucks sounding like a machine gun. Since hen mallards seldom make this exaggerated sound, it's important not to overuse this call. Instead of using the feed chuckle, Gardner prefers to use a mixture of clucking sounds, which hens more commonly make when they rest contentedly on the water.

When faced with ducks that continually circle out of shotgun range, you'll need to change your calling cadence or do something different to convince the birds that it is, indeed, safe to land. Some hunters attach cords to a few of their decoys so that they can tug on the blocks in the hopes that such movement will be enough to convince undecided birds to head to the decoy spread.

As larger flocks of ducks approach your decoys, it's important to keep movement in the blind to a minimum, for it only takes one set of eyes to spot your movement and blow your cover. If ducks appear as through they're about to vacate an area, world champion duck caller Tim Gesch blows a more demanding call by speeding up the cadence and increasing the volume of his quacks. This is the all-important comeback call. Once you've mastered these four calls, you'll be welcome in any duck blind.

I f you kill your limit, spend another hour or two in the blind or pit just watching and working birds. You can learn plenty about waterfowl when your shotgun is empty. It's also a good way to steady a young dog — birds will come in, but there will be no shooting. It teaches him he doesn't get to go after everything and takes a bit of the edge off his intensity. It's also a good time to brush up on your identification skills.

Shop class goose decoys — make them yourself from old tires, a few scraps of plywood, and any leftover black and white paint in your workshop. 1. Using a saber saw or heavy-duty utility knife, cut and remove the metal bead from the inner circumference of each tire side. Then cut the tire casing into thirds; each tire makes three decoys and the natural goose-like coloration of the rubber needs no painting. 2. Draw a representative goose head on the plywood, cut it out with the saber saw, and paint it all black with a white throat patch. You may wish to design some heads in the alert position and some with outstretched necks in a feeding pose. 3. To mount the heads on each casing, drill a hole into the bottom edge of the wood and twist in a short piece of threaded rod; a stove nut and bolt with the head cut off will do. Drill a hole in the casing, push the rod through, and secure in place with a wing-nut. During the off-season, you can remove the goose heads in minutes and stack them on a shelf. The tire casings can be stacked behind the garage. In hunting season, just throw them in the back of your pickup and never worry about their being damaged.

In the late season, waterfowl can become wary of decoy spreads. To encourage ducks to light in your spread, confidence decoys can help. Set three or four large Canada goose decoys about 30 yards away from the main spread. Along the shore, place one blue heron or crane decoy. To draw in those crafty drakes, set your decoys in hen-and-drake pairs since ducks are beginning to form their pair bonds for the coming spring breeding season. If an unwanted duck lands in your spread, let it be. This live decoy is likely to be the deciding factor for suspicious flybys.

Toward evening, set a few dekes in flooded stands of timber. Mallards, blacks, gadwalls, and woodies are fond of these haunts. Move your feet and legs to create waves to simulate feeding ducks. Search the sky with your eyes, not your upturned face.

Fed by groundwater, spring creeks seldom freeze over in winter. Waterfowl are prone to congregating in and near these waters at this time of year.

Expert Advice for Better Decoy Rigs

by Chris Dorsey

THE ART OF DECOYING WILDFOWL IS AS OLD AS HUMAN ingenuity, dating back perhaps 4,000 years. The era of the modern decoy, however, was born with the age of the market gunner during the late nineteenth and early twentieth centuries. Though we deplore the excesses commercial hunting brought about, the perpetrators were nevertheless inventive sorts. They devised numerous ways to take scores of ducks and geese — not the least of which was the use of wooden decoys. The term "blocks" — still often used to describe decoys — stems from the rough forms of the early wooden decoys.

From the excesses of the market gunning days, however, modern decoys have undergone something of a revolution in design. Waterfowlers today have more options for lighter, stronger, and more lifelike decoys than ever before. These modern creations mean hunters can deploy larger spreads in less time. One can only imagine what effort it must have taken to lug a few dozen soaked wooden decoys from a favorite waterfowling hole.

For many waterfowlers — whether hunting ducks or geese — deploying the most number of decoys is critically important. Many snow goose hunters have taken this to the extreme, throwing hundreds of white plastic sheets or rags randomly across a grain field to create their spreads. Such hunters are banking on the notion that the enormous spread will look enough like a flock of birds to keep the geese from looking at any one rag. By the time birds are close enough to tell they've been duped, they're usually within shooting range.

Waterfowling guru Tim Peterson says when it comes to fooling snow geese, it's also important to have enough hunters hidden among the decoys who know how to blow snow goose calls. This defies conventional wisdom, however, because many believe that the deafening call of snow geese, often traveling in flocks numbering into the thousands, is so loud that it would be impossible for them to hear hunters calling from the ground. Peterson's team of hunters who are past winners of the Bottineau Shootout, a contest to determine the best snow goose hunters in North America, has proven otherwise.

Some snow goose hunters, meanwhile, are abandoning traditional rag spreads for more lifelike decoys. Tom Farmer, designer of "Waddler" decoys, sees the trend growing as snow geese become increasingly difficult to decoy. While populations of lesser snow geese have grown at an exponential rate, hunters are taking fewer birds—despite increased bag limits and longer seasons. This stems from the fact that once snow geese have survived a few hunting seasons, they become very difficult to lure to decoys.

The average age of breeding lesser snows on a La Perouse Bay study area, in fact, is an incredible 12 years old! Such birds are nearly impossible to take using conventional methods. Farmer's Waddler decoys are cone shaped creations that attach to stakes shaped and colored like the head of a snow goose. The decoys also wiggle back and forth in even the slightest breeze, hence their name. Wind socks take advantage of gusts, as well, adding movement to a spread with each breath of wind. Waddler decoys and wind socks are easy to deploy, so hunters who want both large decoy spreads and movement can have them.

Mark Higdon, a noted decoy designer, is also convinced that movement in a decoy spread is vital to fooling seasoned Canada geese. His "Finisher" decoys feature flexible heads and legs. By adding several of these motion decoys to a spread, Higdon believes hunters will have an edge over other waterfowlers whose decoys are merely stationary forms. Most Canada goose hunting in America is done near refuges, so the birds often have plenty of opportunity to study decoy spreads continuously deployed by hunters surrounding these refuges. By late season, these birds have seen just about every kind of decoy spread imaginable. Too many hunters also make the mistake of leaving their decoys in the field throughout the season. After associating gunfire with the static spread, geese will soon learn to avoid such places.

If you must hunt from the same blind throughout the season, pick up your decoys after each hunt; otherwise, birds will quickly discern your decoys from live geese. Try to shoot your birds out of small flocks, as well, so you don't divulge the location of your hide to the entire refuge population of Canadas. Many seasoned guides will also rest a blind for a few days each week, varying decoy spreads before each hunt. The best option, of course, is to move to the birds by scouting their movements each day. Canadas routinely return to the site in which they fed the previous day — provided they haven't been spooked from the area.

Goose hunting outfitter and decoy creator Darrel Wise advises that hunters should also position their blocks in small clusters to simulate family groups feeding in a field. Wise does exactly that with his "Real Geese' silhouettes. Also make sure to leave an opening in the center of the spread where approaching geese can land. He deploys his spread under the cover of early morning darkness, having selected the location by patterning the movement of geese the evening before. He shovels out shallow coffin pits in which to wait for the dawn to deliver the honkers. The lightweight silhouette decoys make set up a breeze, and being mobile is a huge advantage to any goose hunter. To be sure, getting under flights of birds that are departing a refuge to feed is paramount to hunting success.

While most duck hunting is done over water, it's still a good idea to pattern bird movements just as you would when goose hunting over land. Ducks often like to frequent different sloughs and marshes at various times of the day. There are, however, several time-honored decoy rigs that will work for either divers or dabblers. These patterns are designed to simulate resting or feeding ducks, and both puddle and diving ducks exhibit unique flock patterns on the water. For instance, diving ducks often feed in a row; therefore, several diving duck patterns use decoys placed in relatively straight lines. Approaching diving ducks often fly directly down the line of blocks, choosing to land at the end of the decoys where hunters should be waiting.

Puddle ducks are often more discerning than their diving duck counterparts — especially late season mallards that have survived a gauntlet of hunters from their northern breeding grounds to their wintering sloughs in the south. Decoys are only part of the equation to successfully take these birds, for calling, hiding, and shooting all determine the outcome of a hunt.

As with any kind of waterfowling, however, finding a spot where the birds want to be is critical. To paraphrase the old real estate axiom, the three most important parts to successful waterfowling are location, location, and location. As with geese, scout duck movements to find a spot where they want to be and set your decoys there, and you'll increase the chances of your decoy spread enticing birds tenfold.

Many puddle duck hunters also like to add movement to their decoys. Some attach strings to a few of their floating blocks so that they can jerk the strings to get the decoys to move as birds fly past. The movement of ripples on the water some-times entices ducks to take a closer look, and it keeps the birds' eyes focused away from you. Some hunters, however, place their decoys too far from their blinds. When the birds do approach, they are often out of easy shooting range. Try to direct the birds closer to guns by leaving an opening in a spread perhaps 25 or 30 yards from the blind. Use a rangefinder to make sure of the distance, for this will help you reduce your chances of wounding and losing birds.

No matter how long you've been waterfowling, never cease studying the birds and their patterns, for such information will give you new insights into better hunting techniques and add enjoyment to your waterfowling experience. By experimenting with your decoy rigs, too, you'll discover the spreads that work best in your area. Such ingenuity has been the hallmark of wildfowlers for generations, and with a little imagi-nation you can add your own traditions to the sport.

When you travel to your duck blind in the early morning darkness and turn your flashlight on, you may experience temporary night blindness when you turn the light off. To avoid this, keep one eye closed when you turn the light on. This will not totally prevent night blindness, but it will reduce it sufficiently so you can see well enough to navigate. Red cellophane over the lens or a red lens will also save your night sight.

Blue-winged teal, all things considered, would really rather have it warm. They are among the earliest migrators in the fall, the latest in the spring, and the last nesters on the breeding grounds.

The population of mid-continent lesser snow geese has grown 800 percent in the last three decades. While spring seasons, large bag limits, and the use of electronic calls have had some effect, the overpopulation of these birds has severely degraded their sub-Arctic nesting grounds.

N ot every shot at a goose is a close one. Considering the ballistics of steel shot, frequent goose hunters need the added punch of a 10-gauge or 3 1/2-inch 12 gauge. The conventional wisdom on steel has been to use shot two sizes larger than the lead shot you used to use. You may also consider one of the other, more expensive but ballistically more efficient options, such as bismuth or tungsten shot.

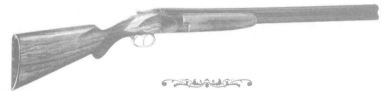

F or an effective, attractive camouflage paint job on your canoe or duck boat, follow these easy steps. First, brush on or spray your clean, dry boat with a good quality paint in a marsh grass or olive drab color. When it's dry, cover about two thirds of the new paint with cattail reeds and spray with flat gray primer. Allow to dry again before relocating the reeds and spraying once more, this time with flat black. The cattail reeds will mask the original paint to create an attractive pattern that will easily blend into the background when hunting.

Calling Canadas

Like ducks, Canada geese consistently employ a series of identifiable calls. Their "language" consists of five calls. The first is the greeting or hail call, and it is to goose calling what the highball is to duck calling. To blow the greeting call, simply say to-wit, to-wit, to-wit into your call. The "to" represents the her of the her-ONK sound made by Canadas. The louder "wit" part of the call is the accented ONK. In addition, many Canadas make a low, growling sound. To mimic this, say grrrit, grrrit, grrrit into the call, varying the loudness until it closely approximates the sound made by the geese.

World goose calling champion and noted southern Illinois guide, Tim Grounds, likes to use the intermediate greeting call when geese have broken away from the flock to take a closer look at your decoys. Here, you'll want to decrease the volume of your call while at the same time increasing the speed of the to-wits to achieve an excited tone. Again, this call can be modified to re-create a variety of varying sounds; just experiment with your call as you listen to live geese.

Most successful goose callers use the cluck or feeding call when geese are approaching the decoys. To make this sound, say twit-it in a series that starts slowly but builds quickly. This call is especially effective when used in conjunction with a growling call.

As with ducks, one of the most important goose calls is the comeback. The call is meant to entice geese to take another look at a hunter's decoys. The call consists of a long, single note with a lonesome, forlorn sound and is the ideal call to use when trying to turn birds away from another hunter along a shooting line. To blow the comeback call, modify your to-wit call to to-wiiiit, to-wiiiit, to-wiiiit.

Finally, the last vocalization frequently employed by Canadas is called the lay-down call. This is an assurance call designed to further convince birds that they've made the right choice by deciding to land near your decoys. To blow the lay-down, stutter the to-wit calls in short, quick bursts of sound and add a growl to achieve the murmuring sound of geese feeding contentedly.

As with any game calling, only time in the field looking at and listening to wildlife will give you the essential experience you need to become a proficient caller. By following the advice of these call masters, however, you'll be amazed at how quickly you can become a successful caller.

Some people ask why men go hunting. They must be the kind of people who seldom get far from the highways. What do they know of the tryst a hunting man keeps with the wind and the trees and the sky? Hunting? The means are greater than the end, and every hunter knows it.
~Gordon MacQuarrie

Migration was a mystery for centuries. Aristotle thought that many birds spent the winter sleeping in hollow trees, in caves, or beneath the mud in marshes. Some people even believed that the birds left the earth. Cotton Mather, a 17th-century New England minister, once said, "The wild pigeons on leaving us repair to some undiscovered satellite accompanying the earth at a near distance." During some slow days on the marsh, we could easily start to think Aristotle and old Cotton may have been onto something.

The traditional way to hunt wood ducks is to shoot the roost ponds. There's no reason to arrive early at the roost; most of your shooting will occur in the last few minutes of legal light. Nor is there usually any need to build a blind. Instead, just lean up again a tree and wait. The first of the wood ducks may not arrive until five minutes before the end of legal shooting time. But be sure to keep an eye on the clock when the action starts so you won't be in violation, and mark your bird well — the low light can make them hard to find.

Successful wood duck hunting begins with scouting the ducks' daily patterns. Watch for them at dusk as they head toward the timber. Typically, wood ducks travel singly or in pairs, and occasionally in small, low-flying flocks. At a distance, you can recognize a wood duck by its long body and tail, the way it holds its wedge-shaped head up in flight, and by the whistling sound it substitutes for quacking. If you spot a flock one night, note the time and wait a little farther along the route the next evening. Eventually they'll lead you to the roost.

Keep your eye on the first duck that you hit, following it all the way down to the water or ground before trying for a second. Pick a fixed landmark to draw a line from you to your bird so you can send your dog, or yourself, straight along it.

Of the world's 147 species of swans, geese, and ducks, about 40 make North America their home for at least part of the year, 20 of those species being ducks. They can be divided into seven primary groups: swans, geese, dabbling or puddle ducks, diving ducks, stiff-tailed ducks, whistling ducks (tree ducks), and mergansers.

Set goose decoys in small family groups, especially early in the season, facing into the wind, toward your blind. Have one head-up sentry for every half-dozen birds for added realism; too many sentries indicate a nervous, threatened flock and may alarm incoming birds. Have a line of "newly arrived" dekes approaching the spread from downwind.

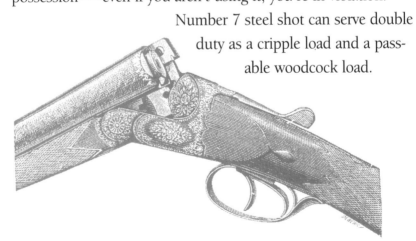

Pattern more than one flock of geese and plan to hunt more than one field over the course of the season. Hunting the same field more than twice a week is a sure way to shy geese away from it permanently.

Duck hunters who wade shallow rivers and streams might want to keep a box of Size 7 1/2 bird shotshells and an upland game vest (hunter orange, if state law requires it) in their vehicles. You never know when woodcock will decide to fill the coverts adjacent to your duck stream. The small birdshot is more economical and delivers a better pattern for woodcock than No. 4 steel shot. Just be sure that when you are hunting ducks, the lead shot is not on your person or in your possession — even if you aren't using it, you're in violation.

Number 7 steel shot can serve double duty as a cripple load and a passable woodcock load.

A Heavenly Encounter

In Spite of growing up in devout Scandinavian Lutheran surroundings, I'm not a deeply religious person. While Mom may remain dismayed by my poor church attendance record, I suspect that at least some of the "rules of life" may have rubbed off on me, sometimes in spite of my best intentions otherwise. However, in 1996, six of us witnessed a spectacle that I have often found difficult to put into words, except as a "religious experience."

The timing of our North Dakota snow goose hunting trip was perfect. It was late October as we set the 1,200 snow goose decoys in the wheat stubble field. The snow fell heavily, and the temperature was only 15 degrees Fahrenheit. An Arctic wind near 30 miles per hour was pushing huge concentrations of waterfowl out of Canada and into northern North Dakota. The resulting migrational phenomena was dubbed the "Grand Passage" by Ducks Unlimited. In fact, the hasty retreat of millions of waterfowl in such a short time caused air traffic control radar operations to malfunction in some of the Midwest airports.

The six of us lying on the frozen ground in the decoys were all wildlife biologists who had chosen waterfowl and wetlands as our area of expertise and focus. We like waterfowl, and we enjoy waterfowl hunting. Mid-continent snow geese populations were already on their rapid ascent, and it wasn't unusual to have one-and-a-half to three million birds staging in North Dakota at one time. Most of the birds can be found staging in the northern tier of the counties on three national wildlife refuges, feeding morning and evening in adjacent stubble fields.The evening prior to the hunt, we scouted the area to find locations where the birds were feeding, knowing that they were most likely to return to the same area in the morning. About three-quarters of a mile from the refuge boundary, we discovered a quarter section of wheat stubble seemingly covered with snow geese from end to end. Arriving back at the location at 4:30 a.m., we quickly set about the task of setting up our spread, and were lying on the ground in our "whites" by shooting time. We didn't have to wait long for the specatacle of a lifetime.

Our hope was that the geese would leave the refuge in small groups, providing a morning of shooting opportunities. What occurred, however, was the opposite. One of the fellows shouted "Here they come!" and I looked toward the refuge to see a huge concentration of birds headed our way. We later "guesstimated" the flock of snows in the neighborhood of 30,000 to 40,000 birds. As they arrived at our decoy spread, they began milling and circling directly above us, just out of shooting range. The cacophony of sound was nearly deafening as tens of thousands of geese swirled above us at 80 to 100 yards. For the next several moments we were mesmerized by the spectacle. The scene played out in slow motion, but probably lasted only 15 or 20 seconds. Then, convinced that our decoys weren't to be associated with, the birds drifted off and landed in a field nearby. For the next few moments there was silence in our decoys as we contemplated what we had just observed and heard. Finally, one of my fellow hunters said, "Oh, my God." We got to our feet and quietly shuffled toward a meeting spot in the middle of the decoys. Not much was said. In retrospect, I believe we were afraid of shattering the moment. Other hunters have witnessed such a spectacle, though not a lot of them. As I reflect on those precious seconds of seeing nature in her most glorious splendor, the thought occurs to me that a nonhunter would never have the same opportunity we had to be exposed to our "religious experience."

To harvest snows, experienced hunters favor extremely large spreads. Two hundred decoys is considered a small set for snow geese. Some guides have been known to put out several thousand decoys. Because of the number involved, paper or "rag" type decoys are used by most waterfowlers. Crumpled up and stuffed in a bag, they weigh next to nothing, yet  fold out on top of marsh grasses, wild rice stubble, or stakes to present a fairly lifelike silhouette to birds flying overhead.

When snow geese come in as close as you feel they are going to, rise up swiftly, pick out a single goose and aim at its head, pulling forward with a smooth lead as you slap the trigger. If you aim at the head but your lead is a bit short, you'll likely hit the breast and still bag the bird. All geese, because of their size, are moving faster than they seem to be, and underleading is a major cause of misses and cripples.

Wind-sock decoys that flutter in the breeze, and kite decoys that provide motion to the spread, are also used to lure in wary snows. Of course these are only effective when the wind is blowing.

H unters over decoys are especially prone to shooting over an incoming bird. As a duck or goose nears, it is dropping, and the angle of its approach increases. Account for this by allowing plenty of lead, which equates to holding under the bird.

T he better you see, the better you can shoot. As the distance to a duck or goose varies, coming closer or getting farther away, concentrate on maintaining focus on that one bird. Failure to do that results in a fuzzy target, making it more difficult to determine range, speed, and angle of deflection.

Extremely important for hitting a target with a shotgun, especially when the target is a duck or a goose, is proper position — of both the shooter and the bird. Anticipation, honed by experience, enables you to fine-tune this requirement. It lets you make your move to shoot as the bird approaches at the right time for that situation. If you move too early, the birds will flare at marginal range. Move too late, and the difficulty of the angle is compounded.

A properly fitted shotgun can be mounted smoothly and easily. It will "point" where the hunter looks with little or no adjustment after the buttstock hits the shoulder. When trying to hit a duck or goose, that proper gun fit can make the difference.

Fun and productive, jump-shooting ducks offers shots that can be easy or impossible. Remember that close range is essential. Shoot above a climbing bird, factoring in any other lead that's necessary. Watch the angle of the retreating duck or goose. As in trap, that "straight away" bird often isn't. When a bird flushes, get your balance before you shoot.

Wild Goose Chase. This saying was derived more from horse chasing than from geese. A wild-goose chase was a horse race in which the horses were forced to follow the leader at fixed intervals, one horse never allowed to overtake another. They eventually became exhausted — hence the idea that a wild-goose chase is an impractical and ill-advised search for something nonexistent or unachievable.

A mallard's field of vision is 360 degrees. This is especially important to remember on birds making a just-out-of-range pass and turning to return. If you shift position or move in anticipation of their return, you'll be spotted.

There is no white meat on a goose. The easiest shots are those made before the bird passes the 90-degree mark. The most difficult: beyond 90 degrees, going away at infinite angles. Remember to focus on the head of the duck or goose when establishing your lead. On overheads, wait until the bird is in range, mount and swing smoothly and quickly, touch it off when the gun muzzle blots out the bird, and keep swinging.

N othing focuses a hunter's total concentration more intently than does the decision to shoot only one bird from a flock. It aligns all the senses on the task at hand: one duck, or one goose; no more. Modern bag limits invite hunters to do just that — shoot no more than one bird from a flock — to lengthen the pleasure. That same focus is obviously the right one to have, even if conditions dictate that you should try for two or even three, since you can't kill a second duck before you kill the first one.

You can decide whether ducks are worth trying to call by how they are flying. Birds that are high up, flying fast and in a straight line know where they are going and aren't likely to come to your spread. Lower birds, however, that don't look quite as purposeful in their flight can often be lured in with a good spread and artful calling.

The basic duck-calling sound is the quack or a dwit sound. Make it by drawing air up from your diaphragm. Control the note with your tongue, and cut it off sharply for an authentic sound. Remember that the duck call is a musical instrument; it takes lots of practice to master.

When wearing chest waders, you'll have a hard time getting keys out of your pants pocket. Many chest waders have a pocket in front for storing small items such as keys, but the danger is that the keys will fall out and you will lose them. You can fasten the keys to the inside of the chest pocket with a large safety pin. Diaper pins work best, if you can find them these days. They are large enough to handle easily, readily accommodate a key ring, and have a protective sleeve over the clasp to prevent accidental opening of the pin.

Ducks on the Water

by Martin Bovey

T HE FIRST MORNING I WAS ALLOWED TO HUNT ALONE WAS also the last time I ever tried to kill a duck sitting on the water. When we heard the first shot that morning, Chuck and I sprinted for the shore of Heron Lake and slithered out over the "boardwalk" to the blind where my dad was shooting. In spite of a good wind not many birds were flying, and I soon grew impatient for action. Furthermore, the idea of being alone with my gun and a pocketful of shells fascinated me, so after a bit I said I guessed I would wander down the shore to see if I could jump a teal or at least pick up a cripple or two.

It was glorious sneaking along through the rushes, and with the Parker in my hand I felt very much a man.

A few teal and a mallard or two that had been feeding in potholes or sleeping on the mud bounced into the air ahead of me, but always they were just out of range. I spotted a fine drake canvasback—undoubtedly a cripple—skulking in the reeds, but he too eluded me. I was becoming discouraged and very weary. It was such tough work pushing through the rushes and dragging rubber boots through six inches of mud or a foot of water that I was about ready to give up and head back for the blind.

Then suddenly I saw something that stopped me dead in my tracks. I looked again. It was too good to be true, but it was true. A quarter of a mile down the shore, on my side of a small island of thick reeds, a big flock of ducks was bobbing about, busily feeding, the sun flashing on their white backs. "Canvasbacks!" Oh boy!

I estimated the distance from the shore. Forty yards. Perfect range. Then I slipped back into the reeds and, moving with the utmost caution, started on a long, curving course calculated to bring me out exactly opposite that splendid flock. Periodically I slowly raised my head and surveyed the situation. My course was correct, and the birds were still there.

For the last hundred and fifty yards I crawled. One boot came half off and filled with water. I was wet to the chin and covered with mud, but at last the wall of rushes in front of me began to thin, and I saw the lake. On it were those busting big "cans."

Flat on my face I wriggled the last five yards. Then I clicked off the safety, very slowly shouldered the gun, tried to point the bouncing barrel at the thickest part of the flock, and pulled both triggers.

Not a duck stirred. But across the water from the island of reeds came a cyclonic roar—the voice of Uncle Charley when he was as mad as anyone had ever seen him. "What the hell are you doing shooting at my decoys? And who in hell are you anyway?"

Utterly crushed, I turned a small, wet, muddy stern in the direction of that great flock of canvasbacks and, with my nose nearly grooving the mud, made my way inland. For two hundred yards I crawled—faster than I have ever crawled before or since. Then I stumbled to my feet, and with my head bent below the level of the reeds I ran.

That was the first time, and the last, that I ever shot at a sitting duck.

To improve your duck hunting, visit a wildlife refuge this winter and listen to the waterfowl calling in the marshes. Practice talking to them and seeing how close you can match your calls to the real McCoys. For the same reason, try your calling out in the spring when the drakes are looking for mates. Take your call fishing with you and quack away at any lonely bachelor ducks. You'll be able to tell when you're doing it right — the duck will almost drop into your boat.

Sales of federal duck stamps reached a peak in 1970-1971 when nearly 2.5 million stamps were sold. Today, about 1.5 million stamps are bought annually by waterfowl hunters and stamp collectors. The youngest artist to ever win the federal duck-stamp art competition was Adam Grimm of Elyria, Ohio, winning in 1999 at age 21.

Setting up for snow geese hunting involves putting out great numbers of decoys, with 600 to 800 often considered a minimum. To ease both the physical and the financial burden of such an operation, hunters have come up with innovative approaches, such as scattering diapers around a field and hanging white plastic flags that blow in the breeze. Some hunters tie rags to a long rope at five-foot intervals, wrap the rope on a big spool, and then drive the field in circles in a truck while someone in the back pays out the rope. The newest wrinkle involves no initial cost. The full-bodied decoys are highly visible to the birds, and can be stacked and carried with ease. Just start collecting five-gallon plastic buckets that are so common these days. Saw them in half, (vertically), using a chain saw, and you're in business. Interspersed throughout your silhouette decoys, flags, wind socks, and diapers, they lend that substantial look so often missing from the birds' point of view.

Safe and proper boat manners are an indispensable part of a hunting retriever's education. Correctly getting in and out of a boat, as well as suitable behavior en route to the blind, are lessons the veteran fetch-dog owner teaches early on, well before his dog's first waterfowl hunt. The incentive, of course: to avoid being capsized in ice waters by an overly-enthusiastic — but inexperienced and untrained — retriever. Boat etiquette is most safely and best taught in warmer weather, with summer weekends or vacations proving ideal times. On a calm, windless day, pick a shallow bay or pond free of distractions, and wear a swimsuit and life vest for safety against possible, and often inevitable, dunkings.

Take along a training bumper in your gear. If things are slow, you can at least give your dog a little action so the day won't be a bust for him. The best time, just in case there's still a chance for ducks to come in, is after legal shooting time as you're picking up. Dogs see a lot better in low light than humans, so he's not likely to lose the bumper.

I f you're a reloader, you've often seen shotshell hulls and bullet brass soiled with dirt and/or mud. To scrub away this unwanted soiling, place the empty brass and hulls in a cloth pillowcase and wash them in your washing machine. After washing, spread them out to thoroughly dry. Be certain they are dry inside and out before attempting to reload them. Restrict your washing to hulls constructed of plastic and brass. Paper hulls, and those with internal base wads made of fiber or paper, will fall apart if you attempt to clean them in this manner.

M any duck hunters early in the season use decoys that are too brightly colored. In the North, the drakes are not that far removed from the eclipse molt, so they are not as likely to be as brightly colored as they will be later in the year. Early season is the time for those dull-colored decoys you forgot to repaint.

In the North, many of the small lakes are clear with sandy bottoms. If you are hunting puddle ducks in shallow, shoreline water, make sure you only use or unwrap enough decoy line to anchor the block. Any more, and the ducks will be able to see the lines from the air, a dead giveaway. You may have to use some extra anchor weight.

Always make sure the water in front of your blind is free of stickups and other dangerous obstructions. When your retriever hits the water with that enthusiasm we all admire so much, things can turn tragic in a hurry unless you're sure the area has been checked out and certified safe.

The Labrador retriever is not only the most popular waterfowl breed, it's the most popular dog breed in the country. The golden retriever is the second most popular dog breed. The Chesapeake Bay retriever, though few in number, is generally regarded as the only "pure" waterfowl dog, being bred for practically no other reason than to hunt ducks and geese.

Remember that steel shot tightens patterns and chokes generally about one gradient: Improved cylinder chokes with lead shot will shoot Modified with steel. Under no circumstances should steel be fired through a Full Choke barrel. Some of the alternative non-toxic loads, however, perform like lead. Bismuth and tungsten matrix loads will pattern as the barrel's choke is marked.

Waterfowl guns should be stocked to shoot a bit lower than their upland counterparts. Waterfowl are often dropping, which means the gun should shoot dead on, placing half its pattern above the point of aim, half below. By contrast, an upland gun, usually fired at rising birds, will pattern about 60 percent above the point of aim, 40 percent below.

When hunting from a layout boat, your gun should have a sling swivel attached to the buttstock. Clip a cord to the swivel and attach the other end to the boat. More than one shotgun has found a watery grave when the boat lurched unexpectedly. And walkie-talkies are a good way to keep in touch with the tender boat.

The Belated Neighbor
by Gordon MacQuarrie

T HE DUST ON THE ROAD WAS SO THICK THAT THE PRESIDENT of the Old Duck Hunters' Association, Inc., was sorry for the dog and almost sorry for me.

Speeding cars raced across that graveled road because it was a connecting link between two concrete highways, and it was a joy rider's October Sunday.

"If I could afford an automobile," said Mister President, wiping his begrimed face, "I would not monkey around driving this road. I would get on one that went to Mississippi or Manitoba, depending on the season."

At the moment Hizzoner was burdened financially and morally with some 60 automobiles including a half dozen super-supers, priced F.O.B. Detroit. Or was it Fling? Memory weakens in the face of the irrelevant. Thank heaven it holds up otherwise.

The Old Duck Hunters', Inc., was trudging back from a fruitless quest for partridge. It had been a fourteen-mile thrust on foot into the southern hinterland of Douglas county, Wisconsin. Rumor, via a helpful neighbor, had spread the word of a partridge plenitude. We found naught but popple and hazel brush.

Well, there we were, we and the poor dog, a springer of excellent coat excepting the ears which never looked any better than grandpa's buffalo cutter robe. About once in so often a car would honk us into the ditch where we would cower until the dust cleared.

"Dang yuh," the old master accused once, "you have picked the leeward side of the ditch three times hand running."

Jerry the springer was smarter than both of us. At the first faint whine of a hill-leaping car he would fling himself deep into the roadside bush. It had been a dry year. It was fierce.

"I often wish I were a dog," the president said wistfully.

We went on. I had a heel blister. He contended I ought to be in better shape because I had drunk the most water at the farmhouse, five miles back. His good spirits buoyed me. Also was I cheered when he summoned me to the center of the road. Pointing to a gravelly, dusty rut he demanded:

"You know what made that track?"

"No sir."

"That's where my tail has been dragging."

A speeder from the rear started us for cover again. As we hit the hazel brush the oncomer slowed and Mister President yelled from his ditch, "Heaven help us, here comes a gentleman! Here's luck!"

The car drew up slowly and dustlessly. The driver was a lone hunting man with a long cheerful nose and a hunting jacket white as sailcloth from many washings. He hailed Mister President.

He was of course a neighbor and brother of the chase. He was also the brother of the chase who had sent the O.D.H.A. on its hideous partridge hunt. The President emerged to make palaver with his great and good neighbor. As in a dream I heard Hizzoner in flagrant fabrication.

"Never saw anything like it . . . Woods alive with partridge . . . Killed a limit apiece . . . Pshaw, we don't want a ride . . . The walk'll do us good . . ."

As the car vanished over a hill I thought of the big bottle of sparkling water I had seen in the back seat.

"I wouldn't ask that scoundrel for the morning dew on his decoys," Mister President snorted. "Did you see him leer at me when I told him about those eight birds we didn't get? He seemed greatly surprised. All I was doing was lying like a gentleman."

Doubtless, I agreed, but insisted I would rather accept one big cool swig out of his water bottle than all the partridge in the North.

This respondent is not one to quibble with our peerless leader. This respondent knows all about the standing feud between this neighbor and Mister President. This respondent recalls the moribund mouse which this neighbor carried in his pocket to a dance. And the itching powder that went with it. And who done it.

The respondent also knows of the time when this suffering neighbor sat for two days on a Washburn County pothole that never saw a duck land in it from one year to the next. And of the slightly turpentined pointer dog, owned by this same victim, and how said pointer embarrassed him before a gallery of the grandest chicken hunters that ever put down a dog on O'Connor's potato field.

"If you ask me," I said, "you are just making trouble."

"Who asked you?"

And now let us forget that partridge chapter and by the license granted to the Old

Duck Hunters begin right away with the plot, the day of reckoning, the Old Man's Method and the ceaseless turning of the spheres in their courses.

It is three weeks later and the Old Duck Hunters are snugly billeted in a familiar cabin on the shore of a big lake shaped like a rubber boot.

The curtain rises on a scene of ineffable peace. The supper dishes are done. Tomorrow's gear is sorted and laid in the boathouse on the beach, including the stable lantern and horse blanket for warming Mister President's shins.

The morrow is one we have marked for our very own. Bluebills fetching through northwest Wisconsin by the thousands. A growing wind rattling the oak leaves. A full moon slicing the clouds.

"It'll blow harder tonight," said Mister President. "The moon is full. Ducks'll fly under the full moon. There'll be newcomers by morning."

"And we'll have the bay all to ourselves."

"Perchance . . . perchance . . ." He was dozing.

And now, music. Music of the foreboding kind, like just before the dagger fight in "Gypsy Love." The back door of the cabin is thumped with tremendous vigor. I hurry to open it and admit the man with the long, cheerful nose — the same who had lured the Old Duck Hunters to the place of Nor Partridge.

Now, I say to myself, the Old Boy will let him have it. He will tell him to his long, cheerful nose what he thinks of him. Now he will walk up one side of him and down the other wearing nothing but a pair of river boots with double-naught corks.

Quickly and often painfully are the illusions of younger men broken. Those two friendly foes fell on each other like long lost brothers. Mister President made the visitor comfortable in his own chair. He offered him extra socks! He commanded me to man the coffee pot for he was a wayfarer in the night and a friend of long standing.

The long-nosed one explained that he was quartered down the lake shore in a neighbor's cabin. He was alone. He had just arrived. He had to get back and put his boat in, fill the motor, look over the decoys. No thanks, no supper, but a cup of steaming coffee . . . well now!

Felicitations flowed like hot fudge. Mister President laid the campaign for Cheerful Long Nose.

"Pshaw, I know these waters like a book. Only place for you to go in the morning is two miles down the shore to the Hole in the Wall."

I wondered if Mister President had lost his mind. The Hole in the Wall is where we were going! And I listened to him saying —

"You get right up there first thing and grab that blind before someone else does."

Long Nose was formally grateful, but it did seem to me that I could detect he had, hours before, decided to appropriate the Hole in the Wall at all costs. He did not say as much. He merely smiled. What you might call the alarm clock smile which says, "O.K. brother. If you set your alarm for 5, mine'll be set for 4!"

He went away and Mister President wound his watch. I protested the division of the Old Duck Hunter's hunting grounds without a vote of the lodge. He merely yawned and set the alarm clock carefully by the faithful hands of the thick gold watch.

Under the covers in the other room I knew what to expect next day — Cheerful Long Nose in the Hole in the Wall blind and the Old Duck Hunters making the best of things on a boggy shore a half mile away. That bog sinks under a man. It is a mere emergency blind. Not a fit place at all for the O.D.H. to carry out the rites in comfort.

We had built that Hole in the Wall Blind. It was ours. Everyone knew it was ours. And he had willed it away without the blink of an eyelash!

The wind was picking up as I fell to sleep. It was crying high in the pine trees. It would be a blustery daybreak. A squirrel scuttered over the roof . . . or was it a chipmunk? . . . mebbe a handful of scrub oak leaves. Then, soon . . . I slept.

"Oyez, oyez! The Old Duck Hunters' Association is now assembled in due form!"

He was leaning over me, a sharp brown eye looking down and a lean brown hand grasping the red blankets. There is no choice at such times. I got up. Better that than to lie there blanketless and shivering.

Breakfast was ready. He looked as if he had been up for hours. There were red spots in his cheeks. They might have been put there by the wind that was fairly tearing the ridge pole off but he said they were "just from leaning over that hot stove frying you four eggs." He was exceedingly happy for a man who had recently given away the best bluebill blind in north Wisconsin.

Down at the boathouse we rolled out the sinews of war and clamped on the motor in a tossing sea. Heaven bless that motor. Not once on the coldest mornings has it failed. Once it spat defiance to a November gale that came upon us with six below zero in the night.

Half way out of our bay I stopped the motor to listen. The sound of no other motor was heard. There was only the long hissing waves and the wind roaring outside my earlaps. I suggested to Mister President that Cheerful Long Nose was already up there, in our blind. He replied —

"What the hell you worried about that blind for? That guy has got an alarm clock that never goes off until it's too late. Head for the Hole in the Wall. If he shows up we'll move out."

In twenty minutes we had made the Old Duck Hunters' favorite setup of bluebill stool. Outside of the fact that I could write a book about it, it is simple: a long narrow horseshoe of decoys, lopsided where one arm of the layout stretches far and inviting into the bay.

"I believe in being neighborly," said the President as we put gear ashore and tucked the boat beneath over-hanging bank willows. "If he comes along we've got to shove over to that bog. Hope your brought your boots."

There was a good twenty minutes to wait before the hands on the thick gold watch declared the legal moment. Long before the moment the bluebills were dive-bombing the decoys. He waited, watch in hand.

Something was certainly doing. Wings were cutting the air to pieces. The light grew and the 'bills increased. Beyond in the tossing bay we saw ragged lines of black. Hundreds of bluebills sat there, over the densest growths of coontail I knew about.

When Mister President said "Now!" it was mere routine lodge work for the association to rise and knock four bluebills to the water from the bundle of six that smashed by.

It is an elegant thing to perform such duties with coordinated dispatch. Among the Old Duck Hunters there is no such foolish: "I'll tell you when," or "You tell me when." Duck hunting men of the veterans' stripe know when, where and how. It is a kind of synchronization with each man taking his allotted side of the bluebill bundle as it swoops at the decoys. It is best done by two who know each other well.

Picking them up fell to the least membership and while I was at it a dozen tried to sit in the decoys.

The bluebill seeker outside of the northern states knows nothing of this; he is inclined not to believe it. His ducks are educated. But let him once see the scaups lesser and greater as they glide into wooden decoys in northern Minnesota and Wisconsin and he will know. Too bad so few know. Too bad, too, that brother bluebill takes to eating fishing foods once he gets down a way into the United States. Up there in the northern tier of states he is just a bundle of jam-packed rice and coontail.

Some of them were big birds. Some of them sat among the decoys. Some of them, shot at, would fly 200 yards away, sit down again and look around to say: "What the hell is this anyway?" Which prompted Mister President to declare —

"One of these days when you're scribbling something just put down that anybody shooting at a bluebill on the water is not only a bum sport but a fool. Anybody who can't hit 'em when they get up hadn't ought to have gone hunting in the first place."

They came from the north and from the west. From Minnesota's northern wilderness, and also from Lake Superior, sixty miles straight north of us, where ducks sit by the tens of thousands until the wind gets at them. As I retrieved them the President speculated:

"One of these here experts told me once that if a bluebill's black head is shot with purple he's a lesser scaup; if it's shot with green he's a greater scaup. Now you just show me any 'bill in that pile, big or little, that hasn't got BOTH green and purple in his black head feathers."

I did not show him. I have gone through it all too many times with the President of the Old Duck Hunters: All I know is what I read in the books and what the Old Man says. Both can't be right. And I have too much affection for the book writers to incite them to battle with the Old Man.

The faithful outboard roared forth many times that morning for the pick-up. Once it was to pick up three canvasback, remnants from a big flock that just cut the edge of our decoys.

"Just what we need," he observed. "There's nothing like a little color to improve the looks of a bag."

By eleven o'clock of that blasty morning we were counting ducks pretty carefully. When the bluebills hit northern Wisconsin in their big years a man with a gun will do well to watch his arithmetic. There is a great difference between ten apiece and twelve apiece. That difference can happen in a five-second flurry. Hence the mathematics, as fixed and certain with Mister President as the hands of his thick gold watch.

The time came for Hizzoner to make a final count and give the signal. He assembled the gear on the shore and I wound in the decoys. Only on the return, facing the bitter northwest wind did I think of Cheerful Long Nose. He had gone completely out of mind in the robust zest of a grand lodge session. Over the motor's roar I asked, "Where'd you suppose he went?"

Mister President shrugged and yelled back, "He ain't got a good alarm clock!"

Battling waves back into our own bay, where it was calmer, I saw on the north shore a tall man leaning over a beached boat. The waves were beating in there hard, for the wind had hauled from west to southwest. The tall man was swooping a pail into the boat. I aimed our boat toward him.

The obvious had happened. The boat he was bailing had drifted away in the night. He was a duck hunter and all such require help. Decoys sloshed in the boat bottom. It was spang up on shore. The wind had been so severe that it had shoved sand up around the boat's bottom and sides. A long green shell case was covered with water.

The man with the pail was Cheerful Long Nose and he was in a bad way. Every time he heaved a pailful of water overside to lighten the boat two pailfuls came inboards.

The President was the first to leap ashore and help. He waded in water to his knees, above the tops of his old gum rubbers. He lugged decoys. He grabbed the shell-box and emptied the water. He just took charge of things and eventually we towed the belated neighbor back to his landing.

"Darned it I know how it happened," Cheerful Long Nose explained. "When I left you last night I loaded the boat and then hauled 'er up on the beach far as I could. Put the motor handy. Had every darned thing ready."

The President of the Old duck Hunters offered him a bundle of bluebill, which he accepted.

"If it hadn't been for you two I never could have budged that boat," he went on. "I've always been careful about hauling boats up high on windy nights."

"Yep . . . ?" said Mister President, more sympathetic than ever.

"But I see now what happened. The stern two feet was in water. The wind rose and sloshed water overside. It got heavy and the boat slid off the beach. I hadn't tied 'er."

"I'll be damned," said Mister President.

We saw him off for the Hole in the Wall. It was full noon with the wind still roaring. He would finish out his bag there, we knew. We gave him hot coffee. We took over six boxes of dampish shells and gave him six boxes of dried ones. He darted out of the bay a happy and grateful man.

The Old Duck Hunters climbed the hill.

"I suppose," said the President of the Old Duck Hunters, "that you think I pushed his boat off the beach."

"Certainly."

He heaved a sigh. He pushed on up the hill burdened with guns and shellcase.

"All I did," he said, "was give 'er a little nudge."

There is no wildfowler worthy of the title who is not convinced of his ability to predict what a flock of ducks will do once it has taken wing. It is a harmless foible. The fact that the prophet is nearly always completely wrong causes him no dismay, nor does it lessen his confidence in his perspicuousness.
~Harold P. Shelden

Early in the season, make sure your shoreline blind or boat blends in with the color. A dead-grass blind against a background of green leaves will stand out like a neon sign.

If you should fall overboard in waders, don't try to swim. Instead, immediately lift your feet as high as you can, floating on your back. Air trapped in the feet of your waders will give you enough buoyancy to stay afloat for a long time. A good habit to get into when boating to and from your blind is to unstrap your waders, thus making it possible to more easily shed them in the event you should have to swim for shore. You may want to consider one of those instantly inflatable vest fly fishermen wear, too.

With the availability of alternative non-toxic shot nowadays, such as bismuth, tungsten matrix, and heavy shot, hunters can again kill ducks and geese at ranges comparable to what lead allowed. However, this is by no means reason to consistently shoot at waterfowl beyond a maximum of 40-45 yards. Consistently putting shot in a vital area on a duck or goose at these ranges is extremely difficult, even for the most experienced of wingshots; most shots at these ranges miss clean or hit the bird too far back, resulting in a cripple. A bird hit too far back, with lead, steel, or any load, will become a cripple, and most likely go unrecovered.

earn to identify your waterfowl. There are restrictions for bag limits in each state so that certain species that are not as abundant as others do not get overhunted. Lesser scaup are a good example — the population has been declining at an alarming rate for a number of years now, so many states have lowered the lesser scaup limit. However, lesser scaup look like ring-necked ducks, whose population is doing fine, and can comprise an entire day's bag. Learning to identify ducks on the wing will help you not to overbag on certain ducks and/or pass up other ducks you could be shooting.

It is always good to have a bag of decoys with extra long anchors — often times you'll find a little honey hole where the birds are piling in, but upon getting there, you find the depth near the blind to be much deeper than your decoy anchors. Long lines on a few decoys can allow you to get to these birds without having to add long lines to all of your blocks.

Having a portable or collapsible blind on your boat will allow easy motoring to and from hunting spots without having to stand to see or go extra slow. It also helps when putting out and picking up the decoys. The permanent high-profile blinds constructed on many boats often prove too unwieldy.

Train your retriever with hand signals and a whistle. Many times during the rough weather associated with waterfowl hunting, the dog is out in noisy wind and surf and can't hear your voice. A whistle can be heard farther. A dog that listens to the whistle and trusts hand signals will be a dog that is out in the cold water, expending as little energy as possible.

River hunting can be great in the late season, especially when other neighboring waters have frozen. However, with the cold temps come ice floes, so mind where and when your retriever goes. Every year, hunters lose dogs due to ice in rivers — the dog breaks through, goes under, and is swept off with the current. Make a reasonable attempt to retrieve your downed birds, but there exists no duck or goose that's worth losing your dog.

High in the sky they make their decision. Wings cup
into parachutes; calling slows, then stops. Steadily,
majestically, thrillingly, the flock falls out of the sky, each bird maneu-
vering in the air currents. This act—
drawing a flock of geese to a set of decoys—
is unquestionably waterfowling's finest moment.
~Zack Taylor

Hide your dog! You go through painstaking detail to camouflage yourself and your boat, then let the panting yellow Lab sit on the end of the blind, in plain view!

When you're sharing a blind with several other hunters, try taking turns at singles, doubles, or flocks that decoy. It's a bittersweet experience to pull up on a drake mallard, touch off a shot, see the bird crumple, then look over to two of your buddies who are reloading, claiming the same bird. And for that matter, avoid hunting with the person who talks a good, ethical game over coffee but blazes away at every duck in sight — if taking turns isn't in his vocabulary, then hunting with him shouldn't be in yours.

When rigging your decoys, if possible, tie anchor lines to the front of some and the rear of others — this will cause the decoys to face different directions when floating, making the setup look more realistic.

Keep spray paint and camouflage tape in your blind bag — oftentimes, when birds are flaring and you're confident they're not seeing you or your dog, and the decoys look fine, what they're seeing is an exposed, shiny part of the blind or an area on the boat where paint has chipped. A quick touch-up can make the difference.

A wild duck is not to be valued in terms of food along with chickens and pork chops. It means day breaking over the marshes and the whistle of fast wings in the gray light. Who can put a price on the sight of black ducks climbing over the willows or pintails setting their wings to the decoys?
~David M. Newell

Shooting at ducks on the water is unsportsmanlike and unethical, but shooting at a crippled duck on the water is necessary, provided that the dog and other hunters are safely out of the way. Killing a duck on the water can be tricky because such a small vital area — the head — is exposed. To increase your chances, aim a bit low — this way, the pellets in the bottom of the spread may ricochet off the water and hit the bird, if the pellets in the top of the spread haven't already done the job.

An invaluable trick to teach your retriever, and one that adds a margin of safety: When your dog is on line after a lively cripple, teach him to stop on the whistle and send him away at a 90-degree angle. When he's safely clear, dispatch the duck with a shot, and send the dog for the retrieve.

A couple of additions to your blind bag: A bird identification guide and binoculars. On slow days, a little bird-watching is a good idea, and the binoculars can help in identifying waterfowl at a distance as well as helping you spot cripples on the water, especially in low light.

P it Boss: Knowing when to call the shot is an art form a waterfowler refines after years of trial and error. When entering a blind, decide who will be responsible for calling the shot when and if birds should approach (tip: let the person with the most experience do it). The trick is "reading" the birds to tell when they have come as close as they are going to get. Too many gunners let flocks of circling ducks or geese pass one too many times before shooting. With each pass, there is a chance that the birds will spot movement, glare off a decoy, or some other clue that signals them to avoid your blocks.

A simple rule to follow is this: The shot should be called when the most number of birds are in range for the most number of gunners. There are, however, variations to this theme. Sometimes, for instance, not all gunners will be in position to shoot — especially if hunters span out across a field spread. In such a case, some gunning is better than no shooting, so realize the opportunity and call the shot. If you stall for the ideal moment, the birds may simply move on without ever presenting the perfect opportunity. A bird in hand . . .

While a duck call in skilled hands can be a musical instrument, blown by an amateur, as the adage goes, it can also be the greatest conservation tool ever devised. The most common crime is calling too much. The golden rule is to keep quiet while birds are approaching and blow when they're going away. The moral: the worst that can happen is that the departing birds will keep on going. With luck, however, they'll turn back for another look.

Every waterfowler has been in a duck blind where someone couldn't resist hacking incessantly on a call. Knowing when to keep quiet, however, has more to do with taking ducks than making noise. If you've got an experienced waterfowler in the blind, take your cue when to blow from him. If you're a guest in another person's blind, it's proper etiquette to ask permission before unleashing your favorite lonesome hen rendition.

Never position your blind facing the morning sun. Coping with light in your eyes is at the very least a hassle, but will certainly prevent you from noticing some approaching birds. Conversely, with sunshine splashing on your face, it'll be considerably easier for passing ducks to spot you.

It's important to be sensitive to wind conditions because birds land into the wind. Position your decoys so that ducks or geese have to pass within shotgun range to land among your blocks — preferably so that the sun is to your back or side. When arranging your decoys, position them close enough to your blind to allow for easy gunning — no more than 25 to 30 yards. It's important to give the birds a landing zone as well — an opening in the spread perhaps 20-30 yards across. Very often the birds will head directly for the "hole," providing ideal shooting opportunities if the opening is placed in front of the blind.

Preseason scouting. Failing to plan, as is often lamented, is planning to fail. While most waterfowlers have a favorite blind they return to season after season, it pays to scout every year, developing contingencies should your once sacred blind go "dry."

Birds will frequent different areas throughout the season. The agricultural harvest, water conditions, and hunting pressure all combine to dictate what the birds will do at any given time. Anticipating what the birds will do is tantamount to gunning success. Since birds like to have a food source nearby their roost areas, try to concentrate your hunting on areas that provide both food and rest sites in close proximity. The trick is to make sure there is a food source throughout the season, for once spilled grains have been eaten, the birds move to new sources.

I f you're hunting Canada geese, it pays to track the grain harvest around refuges so that you can identify the fields in which the geese are feeding. Honkers quickly locate freshly harvested fields, so find a feeding flock in the evening, and you'll stand a good chance of enjoying action in the same spot the following morning (very often on puddle ducks as well). Getting permission from a farmer to hunt his property will be your toughest challenge, but offering to share the bag — in areas where there isn't much hunting pressure — sometimes is enough to convince him to let you hunt. In areas where there is considerable hunting pressure — which includes around most of the major refuges — it often takes a formal lease to secure hunting privileges. Again, if you can afford it, keep your options open by leasing more than one area. Split the cost between several buddies and you'll stretch your hunting dollar.

Weather or Not. The closest I've ever come to meeting my maker has been in a duck boat when the water turned evil. It's the rare waterfowler who doesn't have tales of tenuous boat rides across an unforgiving chop. The Armistice Day storm of 1940 remains as the single greatest hunting disaster of all time. Duck blinds turned to icy graves for dozens of hunters across the Great Lakes states who found themselves trapped by the fury of a surprise blizzard. As the storm descended on the region, many hunters — not knowing the magnitude of the storm — remained in their blinds to enjoy spectacular gunning as every duck in the region seemed to be moving. In so doing, many waterfowlers missed their brief opportunity to make it back to the safety of the shoreline. More than any other, this disaster exemplifies the sometimes seductive danger of waterfowling.

I never voyaged so far in all my life. You shall see men you never heard of before, whose names you don't know, going away down through the meadows with long ducking guns, with water-tight boots, wading through the fowl meadow grass, on bleak wintry, distant shores, with guns at half-cock; and they shall see teal — blue-winged, green-winged, sheldrakes, whistlers, black ducks, ospreys, and many other wild and noble sights before night, such as they who sit in parlors never dream of.
~Henry David Thoreau

Armistice Day Storm

by Gordon MacQuarrie

THE WINDS OF HELL WERE LOOSE ON THE MISSISSIPPI Armistice Day and night.

They came across the prairies, from the south and west, a mighty, freezing, invisible force. They charged down from the river bluffs to the placid stream below and reached with deathly fingers for the life that beat beneath the canvas jackets of thousands of duck hunters.

They will tell you of this for years to come. They will recall how dad and brother were saved, and men who came through it alive together will look at each other with new understanding, as is the way with those who have seen death brush them close.

And eventually they will look back upon it as "the year of the big wind." To such a futile phrase will come what now seems to be the greatest hunting season disaster in Northwest history—and perhaps the greatest in the country's history.

"The dead in this area, 50 miles up and down the river, will likely come to 20 and we know of 16 men," say Winona newspapermen. So much for the statistics, which will be tallied for days as more of the missing are found and more upturned skiffs located.

The winds of hell it was that were abroad that frightful Monday and Tuesday and the winds of hell in high gear with the throttle wide open.

They came, those winds, with little warning of their intensity. After a poor duck hunting season along the Mississippi, duck hunters welcomed the wrath from the west. They liked it in its early stages. They tossed out their decoys and said, "Let 'er blow, that's what we've been waiting for."

They stationed themselves on tiny sand spits and boggy islands and the ducks came. The ducks came with the blast, riding it bewildered and headlong, so many a man, in the first mad hours, took his limit of birds easily. "Bushels of ducks we could have killed," said one survivor. "But we forgot about the ducks..."

Tuesday night on Louis Stantz' boat livery dock, a few miles out of town, 50 skiffs lay at anchor. The dock was snow covered and deserted. Seven dead ducks, frozen stiff, lay there, forgotten. The people who crowded to the dock all day Tuesday had other things to think of. Up the bank from that dock Tuesday came five dead men. The ducks lay there on the dock where the river goes by.

The wind did it. The furious wind that pierced any clothing, that locked outboard engines in sheaths of ice, that froze on faces and hands and clothing, so that even survivors crackled when they got to safety and said their prayers.

The wind did it. The cold was its ally. Mother Nature, sometimes a blue-eyed girl with corn-colored hair, was a murderous mistress Tuesday night on the Mississippi.

She caught thousands of duck hunters on Armistice Day—a holiday. She teased them out to the river and the marshes with her fine, whooping wind and then when she got them there she

froze them like muskrats in traps. She promised ducks in the wind. They came all right. The survivors tell that, grimly, but by that time the duck hunters of the Mississippi were playing a bigger game—with their lives at stake.

By that time men along the Mississippi were drowning and freezing.

The ducks came and men died. They died underneath upturned skiffs as the blast sought them out on bogy, unprotected islands. They died trying to light fires and jumping and sparring to keep warm. They died sitting in skiffs. They died standing in river water to their hips, awaiting help.

They died trying to help each other and a hundred tales of heroism will be told, long after funerals are over.

Over in Winona General Hospital tonight lies Gerald Tarras, 17, a survivor. He is a big boy, nearly six feet, and strong. He had to be, to live. He saw his father, his brother and his friend die. He has not yet come to a full realization of what has happened, for grief is sometimes far in the wake of catastrophe.

Gerald Tarras, his head buried in a hospital pillow, his frost-blistered hands clutching nervously at the bedspread, tells part of it. Just a part. No need to ask him exactly where he was. Just out there on the river. Out on that hideous gut of water between the high bluffs near Winona, where the furies came on endlessly. Gerald tells it hazily, in a sort of open-eyed trance.

"We went out about 10 in the morning, the four of us. It was raining and warm. The wind came at noon. We began to worry. My father (CArl Tarras, 43, Winona) said we'd better go back. It got fierce. Then Bill Wernecke (his friend) died. He was cold. We boxed each other to keep warm. Bill died. I was holding him. He went 'O-h-h-h...' and he was gone.

"We were standing in water. We had a black labrador dog with us. My brother (Ray, 16) died next. Yes, he died. I knew he was dead. He was cold. An airplane flew over and I moved my arm. It saw us. Then my Dad died. They took me off in the government tug and gave me some coffee. They gave me some whisky."

In a Winona restaurant sits Max Conrad, aviator, sipping coffee with Bobby Bean, his assistant. He tells his story very badly, for he is a modest man.

Conrad took a Cub training plane with a top speed of 75 miles an hour and led the government tug Throckmorton and other rescue boats to marooned hunters on the river. He flew all day, sometimes with Bean, sometimes alone.

He would fly his plane repeatedly over a spot where hunters were caught and the rescue boats would know where to go. He would toss out packages containing sandwiches, whisky, cigarettes and matches. He would open the door of his plane and, with the motor cut, shout down to the men below to "hang on, help is coming." He would route the little plane time after time through channels over which marooned hunters could follow in skiffs.

Conrad tells a poor story, for he is modest. Harold Eastman, of Winona, meter superintendent for the Mississippi Valley Public Service Company, tells Conrad's story—and his own—better.

"I was hunting with R.J. Rice and Richard Guelzer. The wind caught us on a bog. The oarlock broke. Dick said 'we camp here.' We turned up the skiff for a windbreak. We tried to light a fire but everything was wet and it was too windy. At 9:30 am Tuesday we heard a plane. We fired our guns. The plane did not see us. At noon the plane saw us. It was Conrad. I know him. He saved our lives.

"Conrad yelled down to us from the open door of the plane: 'Sit tight! We'll get you out of here!' In five minutes he was back with a tin of food and cigarettes and dropped it. He kept flying over us, then hollered down 'start out and go in the direction I am!'

"We took our shotguns and started. Conrad said 'Leave your guns and take the skiff.' We did. We broke through ice several times, then we would hang onto the skiff and work it along the new ice. The Throckmorton picked us up. Conrad saved our lives. I feel all right except for the smoke in my eyes from the fire."

Over at the Conrad home four small daughters, Judy, Jane, Betsy and Molly and their mother waited for their dad. He came home all right. Then he slept hard, for today he took up the patrol again—looking for three skiffs and men, dead or alive.

Conrad says the river shambles was bad because pan ice piled up on banks and islands, so skiffs could not get through. He says he saw dogs alone on boggy islands. He says "the guys who used their heads built windbreaks with their skiffs and then built fires." He says a lot of fellows "lost their head." He is a kind man. He will not even guess at how many are dead. It will take days to find out, he says.

Some of the dead brought in, like those at the Louis Stantz river landing and boat livery, had their faces and hands blue and bruised. It was not possible to park a car at this spot for the cars of anxious relatives—waiting. The bruises, they said, were from the men in the bitter night beating each other to keep warm—shadow boxing and sparring, likely even when their hands were frozen clubs and were without feeling.

Thus they died on the Mississippi on the night following Armistice Day.

Out of town a way is Calvin Volkel. He helped bring in 17. Likely saved their lives. He was sleeping Tuesday night, in the back of his tavern. He awakened and talked:

"At 9 Monday night it began to look bad to me. I needed a good big fast boat to save those fellows out on the river. I was looking especially for Eddie Whitten. I went to town and got Al Squires. We got a 12-horse outboard and started out. It swamped. Then we rowed, each with a pair of oars, shouting to each other 'one-two, one-two' to keep the stroke.

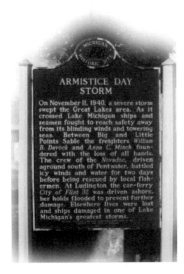

ARMISTICE DAY
STORM

On November 11, 1940, a severe storm swept the Great Lakes area. As it crossed Lake Michigan ships and seamen fought to reach safety away from its blinding winds and towering seas. Between Big and Little Points Sable the freighters *William B. Davock* and *Anna C. Minch* foundered with the loss of all hands. The crew of the *Novadoc*, driven aground south of Pentwater, battled icy winds and water for two days before being rescued by local fishermen. At Ludington the car-ferry *City of Flint 32* was driven ashore, her holds flooded to prevent further damage. Elsewhere lives were lost and ships damaged in one of Lake Michigan's greatest storms.

"Our backs became ice coated. I had put on an aviator's suit. We got to the place I knew Eddie was hunting. There were 16 others there! We got Eddie back ashore, and called the police for help. We needed good oarsmen. The men on the island were lying on top of the fire. Not beside it. On top of it. They lay on top of it!

"They had been shooting off boughs for fuel with shotgun shells. Two men would shoot at once and knock off a bough. I came back and brought off a fellow named Anderson. I brought a hatchet for wood, and whisky. Then we worked it this way. Every man who got ashore in the rowboat went back and took off another, and the one he took off went back and took off the next.

"It was in what we call Dark Slough..."

Also in the hospital is 14-year-old Ray Sherin, whose father, Torge Sherin, was in the rescue party that saved him from the bottomlands death after an all-night search.

The boy has a frozen purplish foot, encased in a special tent. He is not coherent. His eyes stare wildly at the ceiling and sweat stands on his smooth, boyish forehead. He will be all right. His foot may be all right, doctors say. He is very lucky.

Next to him in the room is Bob Stephen, Winona, with a frozen hand. He will be all right. Older, he tells the story that will be told up and down this river for years to come—"the river, the wind, the cold, the fear—and rescue."

Hundreds made it ashore under their own steam and men stood, white and shaking on solid ground and looked back on a river running four-foot waves. They came ashore and home and put down their guns and looked at them hardly believing there was a safe, warm world and they were in it.

There were long prayers by the Mississippi's banks Tuesday, the day after Armistice, when the ducks came and men died.

Dog Gone. When constructing a blind, always build a place to house your retriever. Dogs in the blind are not only a nuisance when they shake water over everything, but they also can be hazardous around guns. More than one gun has been accidentally discharged when knocked over by a dog. A dog outside the blind will present fewer distractions when birds are working as well. Condition the dog before the season to use its own compartment of the blind, and both you and the dog will enjoy greater success.

While rough weather often creates some of the best hunting conditions a fowler could want, it also serves as the temptation to keep people in blinds past the period in which it is safe to be there. Knowing when to head for safety remains a waterfowler's single greatest ability.

Fly over a flock of ducks or geese and you won't see them in any identifiable pattern — no "double-O's" nor "J-Hooks" to be found — so why is it that we've forever been coached to use such spreads? Because history has taught us that they work . . . at least enough times to command repeat deployments. While a decoy spread is designed to coax birds to fly where you want them — preferably in front of the guns — individual blocks are designed to keep birds from landing in certain spots, instead directing them to the open water in front of the hunters. Thus, think of decoys as runway lights for approaching wildfowl.

What constitutes a successful spread? The sarcastic — but sage — response is location. Go to where the birds want to be before concerning yourself with the look of your decoy spread. No manner of decoy position-ing, motion, color, or any other gimmick or gadget is going to overcome the handicap of a place not favored by the birds. The most effective component of decoying, hence, is scouting. In the right location, ducks and geese will come to their shadows.

After you've done your best to find a marsh or field in which the birds want to light, concern yourself with creating the flock effect. Birds aren't lured by any one decoy, but are attracted to the composite of the flock. The shape of a decoy, therefore, isn't nearly as important as the form of the spread. Think random.

Spreads that catch the eye of passing waterfowl look as though they're birds that are resting or feeding — in loose aggregation. Flocks that are alarmed bunch up before swimming or flying away. The best number of decoys to employ is the fewest necessary to entice birds. This is where mobility is important. A handful of decoys in an area where birds want to light is far more valuable than a huge spread in a location in which the birds have no interest in visiting.

I f you're going to sink your time and money into a fixed location, be sure that you stand a good chance of being in a flight lane most of the season. Water and food availability as well as gunning pressure will change as autumn progresses, so anticipate what you're likely to encounter throughout the season. If there are too many uncontrollable variables in any one area, you might be better served by investing in a portable blind set up that can be easily transported to match seasonal bird movements.

For field spreads, consider employing silhouette decoys. They're less expensive than shell decoys or full-body blocks and are much easier to deploy. Many would argue that they're more effective as well, for they have higher profiles than most shell decoys (and some full-body blocks.) This makes them visible from a greater distance, increasing the chance that you'll be visited by passing flocks. That, after all, is the point of the exercise.

Attracting puddle ducks: Where possible, position your blind with the sun at your back and wind such that the birds will have to approach with the sun in their eyes. This will help mask any weakness in your camouflage and any extra movement in the blind. Keep the landing zone opening about 20 yards across and position the center of it no more than 25 yards away from your blind to be certain that approaching birds pass within reasonable gun range.

Even large flocks of geese consist of aggregate family flocks. Position decoys in clusters to represent family units on the ground. Take advantage of even small undulations in terrain to position your decoys in the most visible location. Avoid positioning next to fencelines or other cover when possible, for gun-shy birds tend to head to the middle of open fields. Use low profile blinds to allow you to hunt these open areas. Scout the night before to be sure the birds are using the exact location in which you will place your decoys — confirm by checking for goose droppings.

Divers are predisposed to flying over other of their kind before pitching just ahead of the leading edge of the floc, Take advantage of this habit and position your spread to attract birds to an opening at the end of a line of blocks. Key is to find a point of land near which winds will push moving flocks. Be sure you can safely retrieve any downed birds before setting up.

A Paradise of Wings

by Chris Dorsey

NO MATTER WHICH WAY I TURN, THERE ARE FLOCKS OF pintails dressed in their full nuptial tuxedos. They crisscross the sky in lines, their wings flapping through thermals like the waving legs of feathered centipedes. We're hoping for new birds on the heels of an arctic blast that dumped enough snow to

cover even the tallest cowboy boots as far south as the Texas panhandle just a few days earlier. The sprigs passing overhead are no doubt en route to one of the countless shallow bays that comprise the 40 square miles of Mexico's Lake Guerrero.

Many of these beds are choked with smartweed, one of the most addictive substances known to ducks. In the deeper water, hydrilla is plentiful and the crustaceans that cling to it are preferred by the thousands of scaup, canvasbacks, and ring-necks that spend the winter on this inland sea located just 150 miles south of the Texas line. In addition to the puzzle of pintails above my blind, occasional flights of greenwing, bluewing, and cinnamon teal bank past — mostly going unnoticed until any chance of intercepting them is gone in a blink. Teal don't so much decoy as they appear.

Tilt your head down just long enough to pour a cup of coffee or dry the reeds in your duck calls and teal will often materialize and vanish like birds in some sort of virtual-reality game. Their modus operandi of hopscotching over cattail stands or clumps of rushes as they fly the perimeter of a marsh frequently keeps them hidden until one is lucky to fire even a quick shot in desperation . . . or frustration.

Such was the case for me and my blind mates, Jay Logsdon and Bill Buckley. Logsdon is a veteran waterfowler and a longtime wingshooting outfitter. Buckley is a talented photographer whose waterfowling images have a way of distilling the essence of the sport as only someone who knows the game could capture. Together, we're here to investigate the opportunities that await American waterfowlers and upland-bird hunters — it's a calling in which we are dutifully willing to immerse ourselves.

Despite the abundance of pintails in the vicinity, the birds avoid our blind as though there were a glass dome 80 yards above us. No manner of call or shift in the decoys has any influence on these birds, which have survived hunters from the Canadian prairies to the coastal marshes of Louisiana. And no folks are better at separating ducks from sky than are Cajuns, people who frequently learn to speak mallard before they do French or English.

Resigned that we will have to devise a radical new approach for the pintails, we scan the tops of the dead trees that litter the lake like the aftermath of a firebombing, looking for passing flights of teal. Buckley plucks a cinnamon teal from a passing flock. The bird looks like a feathered ruby coursing through the air — it proves to be one of several of the birds he would take in his five days of shooting both gun and camera. Logsdon and I trip three more bluewings out of a flock that rockets in front, while Buckley gropes for more cartridges. It is a scenario that lasts for two hours — consistent flights of ducks that are the hallmark of Mexican duck hunting . . . and it's what keeps luring thousands of American waterfowlers across the border each year. Logsdon and I climb aboard a small fiberglass boat piloted by Lalo Rubio who will take us to our morning blind. The cold front that passed through yesterday has subsided and there is little wind. The lack of gusts is a mixed blessing of sorts, for nothing improves duck hunting more than blustery weather, but the same breeze can turn a boat ride on the shallow lake into a teeth-rattling adventure aboard a liquid roller coaster. I am content to let St. Hubert serve up whatever the weather and the birds deliver. This is, after all, Mexico, where even poor duck hunts produce more birds than many good days in an American duck blind. I couldn't have imagined, however, the good fortune that was about to befall us.

Before first light, the faint forms of pintails meteoring through the sky appeared, a portent of events to come. No sooner had Lalo and Logsdon finished positioning the decoys than a flock of 20 pintails plummeted from the heavens in a wing-searing corkscrew descent to our spread. It is the sort of sight that reduces even seasoned waterfowlers to something akin to tail-wagging pups. The birds make one last rotation around our blocks before deciding to purchase a piece of calm water inside our spread. Logsdon has other ideas, raising up an instant before calling the shot — it's an old trick every duck hunter learns early on if he wants to assure himself a clean shot at birds that aren't yet flaring from the shots of other gunners. Another secret waterfowlers learn is to watch out of the corners of their eyes for movement from the person calling the shot. The key is to raise up to fire at the same instant the blind boss begins the shooting sequence. It made little difference in this case, however, for so complete was our deception that even a five-thumbed gunner would have had time to unleash several rounds before the birds could make good their escape.

Four stunningly beautiful sprigs fall in the barrage. For a duck hunter such as me who cut his teeth on Great Lakes waterfowling, the sigh of pintails the way artists paint them is like the first moment after opening a gift you've longed to receive. They are a study in perfect elegance — both in flight and in hand — right up to their chocolate, racing-striped heads and bills that look as if they've been airbrushed a gray-blue too brilliant to have come from nature's palette. There is a palpable energy in the blind now as we are buoyed by our close encounter with the sprigs — the same way marlin fishermen toast the first billfish brought to the boat. But the ducks continue to come, another half-dozen pintail flocks surrendering some of their own to our cause. Mixed in between was a flock of some 30 black-bellied whistling ducks, green-winged teal, wigeon, and a perfect mottled-duck specimen — a solitary bird that is only found along the Gulf Coast and that is nearly indistinguishable from its northern cousin, the black duck. It is the sort of rare day when all the forces in the duck world are conspiring to deliver birds to your blocks. It is the memory of such an experience that will forever propel a waterfowler to return to the marsh even after a prolonged dry period. Waterfowlers are nothing if not eternal optimists.